GW00361526

COLLECTING CERAMIC LANDSCAPES

COLLECTING CERAMIC LANDSCAPES

British and American Landscapes
on Printed Pottery

A.W. Coysh and Frank Stefano Jr

Lund Humphries · London

First edition 1981
Published by
Lund Humphries Publishers Ltd
26 Litchfield Street London WC2

SBN 85331 445 4

Designed by Charlton/Szyszkowski
Filmset by Keyspools Ltd, Golborne, Lancs
Printed and bound in the Netherlands by
Drukkerij de Lange/Van Leer BV

Contents

Foreword   by Ian T. Henderson

The china collection of landscapes made by my wife and I started with those printed on popular souvenirs, and *Pictorial Souvenirs of Britain* (1974) was the result of research into this aspect of using landscapes. Mr A. W. Coysh was closely involved with this book and visited the Continent to research the origins of the trade, which also extended to North America.

Mr Frank Stefano Jr in *Pictorial Souvenirs & Commemoratives of North America* (1976) followed the story of Continental export of souvenirs to North America together with those from Britain.

Now Mr Coysh in this book examines the use of British landscapes by Staffordshire potters and Mr Stefano deals with the British and American scenes also used by these potters for the North American market. We hope in due course to complete the story of landscape decoration by examining the work of ceramic artists particularly on Derby and Worcester porcelain wares.

Acknowledgements

For help received in the compilation of this book the authors are grateful to Dr Faith Baver, Mr R. A. Burman of Merseyside County Museums, Mr R. Clements, Mr Robin Gurnett, Dr Richard Henrywood, The New York Historical Society, The Smithsonian Institution, and Mr Gary Stradling.

Special thanks are due to Mr Ian T. Henderson for access to his collection and for his continuing interest and encouragement without which this publication would not have been possible.

Introduction

Two hundred years ago in the potteries of Staffordshire, England, the first tentative steps were made to perfect a printing process which could be used to decorate domestic wares for every-day use. The process was carried out in stages. Firstly, a suitable design was chosen and engraved on a copper plate. A print was taken from this plate on strong tissue paper, using a blue ink, the only colour that would remain unchanged in the heat of the furnace when the wares were glazed. The print was then transferred to the wares from the paper. Finally, the design was covered with a glaze to protect it from wear. In this way dinner and tea services could be produced at a reasonable price and a vast new market was opened up for Staffordshire earthenwares.

In the experimental days at the end of the eighteenth century designs were adapted from those on Chinese imported porcelain, using line engraving. In the early 1800s, however, finer transfer paper became available and it was possible to use some stipple engraving for more delicate work. Landscapes could be engraved with cloud effects and with reflections in water. At this time there was a great deal of interest in distant places. Every well-to-do young man made the 'Grand Tour' through France and Italy to the eastern Mediterranean and he often took an artist with him to record the architecture and scenery. Soldiers, administrators and traders were establishing British influence in India and wrote home about the Hindu palaces and temples, and the Muslim mosques, or about the strange field sports in which they were able to engage, hunting animals unknown in Britain. Artists brought back drawings of these scenes which were published in book form and thus became available as sources for ceramic designs, for there were no copyright laws in those days. For some years, therefore, the prints on dinner wares were of Italian, near-Eastern or Indian scenes.

During the Napoleonic Wars travel in Europe became hazardous and trade with Europe contracted. However, other influences had been at work. William Gilpin, a Hampshire vicar, produced a series of books on the scenery of Britain, illustrated by his own aquatint drawings. This helped to focus attention on the picturesque aspects of the British landscape. Even the caricature of Gilpin in a series of verses by William Coombe, illustrated by Thomas Rowlandson, entitled *The Tour of Dr Syntax in Search of the Picturesque* gave Gilpin's ideas popular currency.

People began to look with new eyes at the British countryside. Roads were improving and artists travelled around sketching country houses, rivers and bridges. A flood of topographical books appeared – *The Antiquities of Great Britain*, *Select Views of Great Britain*, *Beauties of Britain*, *Wales Illustrated* and *Scotland*. All these contained prints which could be adapted by the potters to decorate their dinner services. Between 1815 and 1830 many superbly engraved and printed landscapes of the British countryside appeared on their wares. Many were exported to North America but the potters soon decided to decorate their export wares with American scenes. They were printed in a dark blue and sent in shiploads to ports along the Eastern seaboard from Montreal to New Orleans. As experience was gained, fresh colours appeared – sepia, pink and green prints became popular.

All the landscape wares produced in the first half of the nineteenth century are keenly collected today. Rightly so, for they are cooperative works of art, each reflecting the skill of an artist, an engraver, a printer and a potter. Moreover they have intrinsic historic interest for so many of the old buildings depicted have disappeared or been engulfed by urban sprawl. The collection made by Ian T. Henderson, who has made this book possible, embraces an even wider field, ranging from finely painted landscapes on porcelain to landscapes printed on popular souvenirs which flooded into Britain from Germany in the 1880s. (See his *Pictorial Souvenirs of Britain*, 1974).

The story is never ending. While the Germans were invading the British market, the famous firm of Wedgwood, which had not engaged in the earlier export of blue-printed wares, decided to produce a souvenir pitcher for the US Centennial Fair of 1876 in Philadelphia. This proved to be the beginning of another regular trade in souvenir printed wares to America. In 1906 Wedgwood established an office in New York and by 1950 was producing series of landscape scenes for leading departmental stores. The trade continues in a slightly different form. The pottery used for the souvenirs of 1976 – the Bi-centennial celebrations of American Independence – were in jasperware.

Chapter 1 Transfer-printed Landscapes of Britain

Transfer printing as a form of decoration started by the enamellers of Battersea and Bilston was employed by the Worcester factory on ceramics in the 1760s. Essentially it involved engraving a design on a copper plate and then making prints from this plate on thin paper using a special ink. The printed paper was then applied to the glazed ceramic surface leaving the transferred design as decoration. Heating 'fixed' the print.

The advantage of transfer printing was obvious. Many prints could be taken from a single copper plate and the transferring process could be carried out with relatively unskilled labour.

The Worcester factory used some delightful prints on their wares. Henry Sandon in his *Illustrated Guide to Worcester Porcelain*, 1969, (Plate 37) illustrates what must be one of the earliest of transfer-printed scenes. It shows a young girl drawing water from a well and talking to a shepherd whose sheep stand quietly beside them. Some of these early printed scenes on porcelain were based on the paintings of such artists as Thomas Gainsborough and Luke Sullivan; however they are not landscapes of particular places.

The firm of Sadler & Green in Liverpool was also using transfer printing on ceramics in the second half of the eighteenth century at their 'Printed Ware Manufactory' in Harrington Street, to which several Staffordshire potters, including Josiah Wedgwood, sent wares for decoration. By 1800 transfer printing on pottery and porcelain had spread to factories all over the country.

One of the earliest identifiable landscapes to appear on pottery was printed in Leeds. This was a view of Fountains Abbey, less than 25 miles from Leeds Old Pottery. The abbey was founded in 1132 by twelve Cistercian monks from York who were given the land by Archbishop Thurston of York as a challenge, for the abbey they were to build was to be sited in what was then wild forested country. The handsome tower seen in the print is Perpendicular in date. It was added by Marmaduke Huby, abbot from 1494 to 1526, who made no attempt to live a simple Cistercian existence as did his predecessors. He cheerfully forsook the life of humility, rode about in a coach and entertained his friends lavishly on roast beef and beer. The days of the abbey ended in 1539 and it was later acquired by John Aislabie (1670–1742) who linked the building with his own property of Studley Royal and in 1720 laid out some fine gardens around the ruins. It became a 'show-place', as it is today under the Department of the Environment. This was, therefore, a most appropriate land-

Fountains Abbey, Yorkshire
Plate (c. 1780) of pale creamware transfer-printed on glaze in red. The words 'Leeds Pottery' appear in the print. Diameter 9.9in (25.1cm).

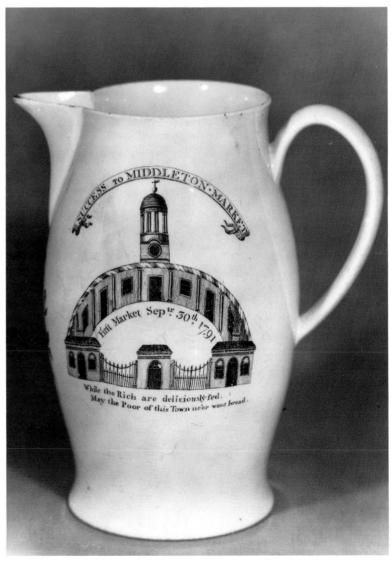

Middleton Market, Lancashire
Creamware jug (1791) transfer-printed overglaze in black. Unmarked. Probably of Staffordshire origin. Height 9.5in (24.1cm).

scape to appear on an eighteenth-century Yorkshire-made dinner service and the transfer work was well executed. Donald Towner in his book on *The Leeds Pottery*, 1963, describes the view as 'one of the best drawn and artistic of all Leeds engravings'. It was thought at one time that the view might be just one of a series of views of Yorkshire abbeys, but so far no other examples have been recorded. It could be that such pieces are from a single specially commissioned service; they may even have been produced as souvenirs.

Most of the landscapes on Staffordshire wares printed by Sadler & Green in Liverpool, and on the wares of the Liverpool Herculaneum Pottery are not identifiable. The most notable was a 'farmyard' scene said to have been based on a cartoon by James Akin, of which there are many versions, on creamware jugs. However, an actual English building, though hardly a landscape in the accepted sense of the word, appears on a creamware jug dated 1791 to mark the opening of the newly built Middleton Market in Lancashire.

Aiken's Description of the Country from thirty to forty miles around Manchester, 1795, refers to the rapid growth of the village of Middleton.

> 'Many buildings have been erected and a grant from the crown was obtained in 1791 for holding a weekly market, and three fairs annually ... for the sale of all kinds of cattle, goods and merchandise, etc., and for the accommodation of those who resort thither, Lord Suffield has, at a very considerable expense, erected warehouses, and an elegant market house, as well as shambles adjoining. The market, though in its infancy, is well supplied with butcher's meat and other provisions.'

These facts are confirmed in Moule's *English Counties*, 1838, which refers to the market house and extensive shambles erected by the late Lord Suffield at his own expense.

Other jugs of this kind printed in Liverpool bear prints of actual places in England as well as in America. One Herculaneum Pottery jug, dated 1810, marks the fiftieth anniversary of the Jubilee of George III's Coronation. It shows Pembroke Place, Liverpool with the statue erected in his honour.

If printed wares were to be subjected to heavy wear the print had to be protected. This could only be done if the printed design could be covered with a film of glaze. The problem had always been to produce a printing ink which would stand the high temperature of the furnace which fixed the glaze. This was solved by using zaffre, a blue material produced by roasting an ore of cobalt, which kept its colour under conditions of great heat. For these wares, the print was transferred to the biscuit before glazing.

As a result of these technical advances, a vast new market was opened up for blue-printed earthenware dinner services. The middle classes who were unable to afford expensive porcelains were able to equip themselves with fine tablewares at a reasonable cost. The early years of blue printing from about 1780–1810 were mainly experimental. One of the difficulties arose from the fact that the transfer papers were apt to tear. However, early in the nineteenth century, a thin strong paper was produced by Messrs Foudrinier who set up a paper mill in Staffordshire to supply the potteries with transfer paper. This made the use of finer engravings possible and by about 1815 beautifully engraved landscapes, using a combination of line and stipple, were being used by some of the larger firms. The quality of the work may be judged by studying the landscape printed on the dish by John & Richard Riley of Burslem. It shows Denton Park, Yorkshire, in its parkland with ornamental trees, a herd of deer and a lake. Note how well the engraver has been able to cope with cloud effects, perspective and the reflection in the water. Such landscapes were framed by decorative borders, usually of flowers, fruit and scrolls.

The manufacture of printed wares involved a sequence of operations employing a number of different workers. A failure to maintain standards at any stage could ruin the final product. The operation is described in detail in the *Penny Magazine* for May, 1843:

'The design, when finished, is given to an engraver, who engraves it on a flat copperplate in the usual manner. From the plate so engraved, impressions are taken upon a peculiar kind of thin paper, made expressly for this purpose by Messrs. Foudrinier. The colour, for the impression, is a mixture of certain metallic oxides with oil, and is brought to the thickness of cream. The engraved plate is placed upon a flat stove and, when heated, the printer rubs the ink well into the device. With a knife he then scrapes off the superfluous ink from the surface, and rubs the plate quite clean, leaving the ink only in the engraved device. Meanwhile the paper has been moistened in soap and water; and an impression is then taken by means of a small roller-press.

Immediately that the printed paper is ready, it is handed to a woman called a "transferrer", who lays it down upon the plate or other earthenware vessel which is to be printed. Sometimes it can be put on in one piece; while at other times it is cut into a few pieces by another female, and then adapted to the various curvatures of the vessel. The transferrer next takes a kind of rubber, formed of a roll of flannel wrapped round the end of a stick, and rubs the paper very forcibly down upon the vessel, the coloured surface being next to the vessel; this rubbing is so violent, that if the paper were not of a tough quality (though thin) it would be worn into holes. The ware, being in the porous "biscuit" or unglazed state, imbibes the colour from the paper. The vessel is immediately handed to

Denton Park, Yorkshire
A typical blue-printed landscape using a combination of line and stipple engraving in the centre of a meat dish (c. 1815–28) by J. & R. Riley of Burslem. Length of landscape 9 in (22.9cm) within a dish 14.6in (37.1cm).

another female, who immerses it in cold water, and washes off all the paper from the surface. It is then seen that the ware has imbibed the colour so intimately that the washing away of the paper has not removed it from the ware; the device is perfectly transferred. The ware is placed in a kiln to drive off the oil from the ink; and the printed vessel is then ready for the process of glazing.'

The Penny Magazine refers to the gradual appearance of printed landscapes:

'In the early stages of the system no fine lines were introduced into the design; but coarse unmeaning patterns such as the 'willow' pattern were alone employed. By degrees, however, a better taste prevailed, and landscapes and other pleasing subjects were introduced.'

At first the potters looked for foreign subjects for their patterns, basing their engravings on the illustrations from books. Spode based a series of patterns on drawings by Samuel Howitt in Thomas Williamson's *Oriental Field Sports*, 1805, and another on Luigi Mayer's *Views in the Ottoman Empire, mainly in Caramania*, 1803. Herculaneum Pottery used T. and W. Daniell's *Oriental Scenery and Views in Hindoostan*, 1795–1807, a source also used by J. & R. Riley and John Rogers and Son.

Monk's Rock, Tenby
Dish (c. 1820) in medium blue by
unknown maker. Length 16.2in
(40.6cm)

Slowly, however, British landscapes began to appear on blue-
printed wares and became very popular after the Napoleonic
Wars when a large export trade developed in Europe and
particularly in America. Ship loads of dinner services were
sent to the East Coast ports of North America from Montreal
to New Orleans. Some were distributed by agents; others
were sold on the quayside. The trade was enormous and a
number of Staffordshire firms specialised in export wares.
Many had specially engraved American scenes (see Chapter
2) but those with British landscapes were equally popular.
The bulk of blue-printed wares with British landscape
patterns were produced between 1815 and 1830. Most
Staffordshire potters were involved in their production and
the enormous range of views used can be seen in the check list
(Appendix 1).

Most of the landscapes were based on engravings in books
published between about 1790 and 1820. The view of Tenby
on the large dish with floral border, for example, was taken
directly from *Select Views in Great Britain* engraved by
S. Middiman in 1812.

A comparison with the actual engraving reveals how very
closely the print on the dish corresponds to the original,
though slight changes were necessary to adapt the rectangular
original to provide a picture for an oval dish. This process of
adaptation needed special skills and many of the smaller

potteries preferred to obtain their copper plates from one of
the many workshops of artist-engravers rather than employ
workers of their own in this specialist field.

A study of these British landscape wares is best made by a
reference to individual pieces which are here presented
alphabetically according to locality. Some bear only a maker's
mark, some a cartouche with the name of the scene, and
occasionally both the scene and maker's name are combined
within a printed cartouche.

Audley End House, near Saffron Walden, was built on the
site of a Benedictine Abbey. It is a large Jacobean mansion,
originally laid out on an extensive scale between 1603 and
1616 by Thomas Howard, first Earl of Suffolk. In 1669 it was
bought by Charles II and it became a royal palace until 1707
when it returned to the Suffolk family. The original building
had two large courtyards but on the advice of Sir John
Vanburgh the outer courtyard was demolished in 1721 and
other structural changes were made later though these kept to
the Jacobean style. Great attention was paid towards the end
of the eighteenth century to the grounds around the house.
Robert Adam designed various structures to enhance the view
and the park itself was laid out by Capability Brown. Among
the Adam buildings are a Palladian bridge (1782–3) and an
obelisk (1774), sometimes called the Springwood column,

which was dedicated to Lady Portsmouth. Both of these appear on the dish. The Temple of Concord (1790–1) designed by Robert Furze Bretlingham to commemorate the restoration to health of George III, may also be seen to the right of the main house.

The full history of the house, now controlled by the Department of the Environment, is given in William Addison's *Audley End*, 1953.

Cambrian Bridges, Denbighshire
Mug (c. 1820–30) by unknown maker. Height 4.8in (12.2cm).

This mug has a printed mark – 'Cambrian Bridges'. It shows the aqueduct which carries the Ellesmere Canal across the Dee at Cysyllte, about four miles south-east of Llangollen. This structure has nineteen stone arches and carries an iron trough 1,007 ft. long at a height of 127 ft. It was designed by Thomas Telford (1757–1834) and was completed in 1805. It attracted a great deal of attention for a generation and was described by George Borrow in *Wild Wales*, 1852. Sir Walter Scott praised it as the greatest work of art he had ever seen. Robert Southey, as Poet Laureate, wrote the following lines in praise of the engineer:

Telford it was by whose presiding mind
The whole great work was planned and perfected;
Telford who o'er the vale of Cambrian Dee
Aloft in air at giddy height upborn
Carried his Navigable road, and hung
High o'er Menai's Strait the bending bridge;
Structures of more ambitious enterprise
Than Minstrels in the age of old Romance
To their own Merlin's magic lore ascribed.

The 'bending bridge' across the Menai Strait was also a subject for a blue-printed landscape.

Cambridge : King's College
Sauce boat stand (c. 1820–30) by
Charles Harvey & Sons of
Longton. Length 8.5in (21.6cm).

The view shown in the print is from the west bank of the
Cam and shows the west front of King's College Chapel
which was completed in 1575 and Gibbs Building designed
by James Gibbs and built between 1723 and 1729. Fine lawns
run down to the river which is spanned by a bridge built in
1819 to replace an earlier bridge which was placed in a
different position. This was part of a landscaping scheme. It is
interesting to note that the boat on the Cam is being drawn by
a horse walking on the river bed.

Many of the localities are named on the base of the wares,
each maker using his own particular cartouche or descriptive
symbol. In this case the view is simply described as
'Cambridge'.

Chepstow Castle, Monmouthshire
Indented dish (c. 1825–35) by
Pountney & Allies of Bristol.
Length 12.9in (32.8cm).

Chepstow Castle, once known as Strigail Castle, stands on a
limestone crag above the River Wye. It was built in 1067 by
William FitzOsborn, Earl of Hereford, as a wooden fortress.
The Norman keep was constructed on the site some fifty years

later and further additions extended downhill. In the fourteenth century a heavy gate was added with a parapet over the entrance supported by an arch springing from between two drum towers.

The castle has a history of death and imprisonment. Edward II was at Chepstow prior to his capture and death at Berkeley Castle. The father-in-law of Edward IV was taken at Chepstow and later executed at Kenilworth.

During the Civil Wars of the seventeenth century Chepstow Castle changed hands several times. The most significant occasion was when Nicholas Kemys of Caldicot captured it for the Royalist cause. The town of Chepstow was held by Cromwell but the castle held out for some time. Eventually it fell and Kemys died in the last battle. In 1655, Jeremy Taylor, the King's Chaplain, was imprisoned at Chepstow.

Perhaps Chepstow's most famous prisoner was Henry Marten who was a fervent egalitarian anxious to abolish not only the monarchy but also the House of Lords. He signed the death warrant of Charles I and when the monarchy was restored in 1660 he was brought to trial and imprisoned for life.

He spent twenty years in Chepstow Castle in a suite of rooms where he was attended by his own servants and was able to receive his family and friends.

Dalberton Tower, Caernarvonshire
Plate (c. 1825–30) by an unknown maker. Diameter 8.6in (21.8cm).

Dalberton Tower is obviously Dolbadarn Tower, still to be seen, near Llanberis in Caernarvonshire. This ancient circular building is one of the stone-built Welsh castles sited in the Pass of Llanberis in North Wales. It is known to have been occupied in the sixth century. There are other similar castles in the area at Dolwyddelan, Aberffraw and Bere. Unlike the castles built by the Normans, which were sited in places suitable for settlement and tended to become the nuclei of large towns, the Welsh castles remain isolated. Dolbadarn is less than a mile from Llanberis, close to the edge of Llyn

Peris under Snowdon. These towers played an important part in the defences of the mountain districts; Dolbadarn was several times besieged in the reign of Edward I.

The pattern is one of a series which included Kirkham Priory, Yorkshire. Occasionally, the transferrer applied the wrong printed name to the base so that views of 'Dalberton Tower' have sometimes been found labelled as 'Kirkham Priory'. Examples have been noted with an impressed crown which is attributed by some authorities to Middlesbrough Pottery but there is no evidence to support this conclusion. Examples appear to be of earlier manufacture, prior to 1834 when the Middlesbrough Pottery was founded.

Dunolly Castle, near Oban, Argyllshire
Mug (c. 1837–50) in medium blue by John Meir & Son of Tunstall. The printed mark includes the series title 'Northern Scenery', the maker's initials J. M. & S, and the locality of the landscape. Diameter 5in (12.7cm).

Dunollie Castle (to give it the modern spelling), now in ruins, is about a mile north of Oban on a bold promontory overlooking the bay. The remains of this ancient stronghold of the Macdougalls include a courtyard of which the keep probably formed one side. The approach was by a steep ascent from the neck of an isthmus which was once cut across by a protective moat. This can be seen on the print as can the *clach-a-chow* or Dog's Pillar, a solid pillar of rock behind it. The name is derived from the legend that Fingal the mythical giant used the rock as a stake to which he bound his celebrated dog Bran.

A building which perhaps attracted more attention than any other in the years between 1800 and 1825 was Fonthill Abbey in Wiltshire and it is not surprising that it should appear on the blue-printed wares of a number of potters, including Adams, Clews, Hall, Stevenson and Wood. It was the brainchild of William Thomas Beckford (1759–1844). Beckford had large estates in the West Indies which depended on slave labour. He was rich, even as a young man. He was also impatient and volatile and was involved in a number of

Fonthill Abbey, Wiltshire
Indented eight-sided dish (c. 1820)
by J. & R. Clews, medium blue
with a floral border. Length 17in
(32cm) Width 12.9in (32.8cm).

scandals which excluded him from polite society. Nevertheless, he had talents and taste and devoted much time to writing and collecting.

In 1793 he approached James Wyatt, the architect, about a scheme he had to build a Gothic structure which would be like a mediaeval monastery. As time passed his plans became more and more ambitious. In 1796 Wyatt produced the design. The building was to have as its main feature a tower 250 ft high. In the following year work started, though the scaffolding round the partially built tower collapsed on two occasions.

By 1800, the building was still incomplete but Beckford, no doubt anxious to establish his social respectability, planned for a visit by Nelson and the Hamiltons, which was to end in a magnificent banquet in the Gothic Hall of the abbey on 23 December before their departure on Christmas Eve. They arrived from Salisbury on 20 December after Nelson had received the freedom of the City. James Wyatt was present and so was Benjamin West, President of the Royal Academy.

There were many delays in completing the scheme, partly due to the dilatory attitude of Wyatt. The building was not completed until 1813. Great care had also been taken over the setting. The abbey stood in an estate landscaped with avenues and groups of trees, the whole enclosed within a wall.

Within the next ten years Beckford faced financial disaster with the abolition of the slave trade. He was forced to sell his collections by auction and he sold the abbey to John Farquhar for £300,000 and moved to Bath in 1823.

In 1825 the great tower of the abbey collapsed, an event witnessed by only one man. The ruins lay virtually untouched until 1844, the year of Beckford's death.

The full dramatic story of Fonthill is told in H. A. N. Brockman's *The Caliph of Fonthill*, 1956, and Boyd Alexander's *England's Wealthiest Son*, 1962.

J. &. R. Clews produced two blue-printed landscapes of Fonthill both framed in the same border. Their Cobridge

Fonthill Abbey, Wiltshire
Plate (c. 1820) by J. & R. Clews, medium blue with a floral border. Diameter 10in (25.4cm).

Pottery in Staffordshire operated from *c.*1815, so assuming that the wares were made and printed before the tower collapsed in 1825, they can be dated to within the 1815 to 1825 period. The view is from the south-west and corresponds closely (except for the disposition of the trees) to a view drawn by George Cattermole.

Cathedral Church of Glasgow, Lanarkshire
Indented dish (c. 1825–30) marked 'Antique Scenery' on lower side of rim. Combed base. Length 19in (48.3cm). Width 15in (38.1cm).

There was an earlier church on the site of the present thirteenth-century cathedral of St Mungo in Glasgow which was also associated with the saint. When the present church was founded by Bishop Bondlington it followed the two-level arrangement of the eastern arm of this earlier building and this gave the designer an opportunity to create a lower church of unusual dignity and splendour in which St Mungo's shrine could be made more accessible to increasing numbers of pilgrims.

Dish (c. 1820–30) attributed to
Elkins & Co. of Lane End,
Staffordshire with the
characteristic border and cartouche
associated with a group of
landscape wares. Length 10.9in
(27.7cm). Width 8.5in (21.6cm).

Jedburgh Abbey in Roxburghshire was founded by David I
of Scotland in 1118 and some good twelfth-century work
remains to this day including the west façade. It was
originally used for monks who were canons – regular or
Augustine friars, brought from Beauvais in France. In
common with other monasteries near the border, it suffered
severely in the English invasions, and from a two-hour long
exposure to the artillery of the Earl of Surrey at the storming
of Jedburgh in the reign of Henry VIII. At the Reformation,
when it does not appear to have been inhabited, the abbey
lands were converted into a temporal lordship, with the title
of Lord Jedburgh. Later they passed to one of his
descendants, the Marquess of Lothian. The building was
restored by the ninth Marquess (1833–1900) who succeeded
in 1870. He was the Secretary of State for Scotland in Lord
Salisbury's administration between 1866 and 1892.

The dish is attributed to Elkins & Co. of Lane End which
was sometimes described as Elkin, Knight & Elkin, a
partnership which operated from about 1822 to 1830. Wares
with similar scenes, identical borders and a similar cartouche
have been noted with the impressed mark 'Elkins'. There
were, however, many partnerships which included the Elkin
family operating in Staffordshire at this time and it is
impossible to be certain which Elkin firm made these
landscape wares.

Lancaster, Lancashire
Eight-sided dish (c. 1814–36) by
John Rogers & Son. Impressed
mark 'Rogers'. Length 20.8in
(52.8cm). Width 15.9in (40.4cm).

Lancaster
Plate (c. 1820) by the Herculaneum
Pottery, Liverpool. Diameter 10in
(25.4cm).

Lancaster seen from the river bank
today.

Lancaster seems to have been a favourite landscape for
makers of the blue-printed earthenware. Four makers portray
exactly the same views except that they all use different
foregrounds and borders.

The foreground used by John Rogers & Son has three
horses, that used by Elkins & Co. has three figures, and a
Herculaneum pottery version also has three figures. The floral
borders used respectively by Rogers and Elkins & Co. are
very similar.

It is still possible to find the place near the river bank from
which this view was originally seen.

Linlithgow Palace, West Lothian
Indented plate (c. 1820–40) by
unknown maker, with floral border
clobbered over the glaze with
green, red and yellow enamels.
Diameter 9.6in (24.4cm).

Linlithgow Palace is sometimes referred to as Linlithgow Castle because, although it is essentially a domestic building, it was built to look like a castle with gun-posts, parapets and massive walls with few windows. The nucleus of the palace seems to have been a tower or fort built by Edward I. The earlier building was destroyed by a fire in 1424, and it was rebuilt as a massive quadrangular edifice on an eminence above a small lake.

In a room on the west side, Mary Queen of Scots was born on 7 December 1542. The north side of the quadrangle was rebuilt by James VI of Scotland after he had also become James I of England following the union of the two countries. The building was done under the direction of the King's Master Mason, William Wallace.

During the uprising of 1745, Henry Hawley, the English Commander-in-Chief, quartered his dragoons in the palace on the night of 31 January 1746 and they reduced it to a ruinous condition.

This plate shows a distant view from across the lake. The maker is not known but it is one of a series which carries a floral border often clobbered with coloured enamels. The quality of all the pieces examined is very high. They include unusual views of Lynmouth, Monmouth, the Powder Mill, Hastings, Richmond, and Thorp, Derbyshire. In each case the scene is named in a panel enclosed by small circles.

Who made these wares? The only clue is that some later blue-printed wares use the same surround of small circles around the words 'Pratt's Native Scenery'. Could the maker be F. & R. Pratt & Co. of Fenton, Staffordshire and, if so, why did the firm fail to include its name on the wares? A possible explanation might be that they also supplied other firms with copper plates from their engraving shop. Minton's are known to have omitted their name from blue-printed wares while they supplied other manufacturers. One can at least be sure that Felix Pratt had had considerable experience of transfer printing before he exhibited colour-printed wares at the 1851 Exhibition. It seems certain that between the foundation of the firm *c.* 1818 and 1851, the firm must have made blue-printed wares which engaged the attention of practically every potter in Staffordshire.

View of London
Dish (c. 1820–30) by T. & B. Godwin with gravy channels and a floral border. Maker unknown. Length 18.7in (47.5cm). Width 14.3in (36.3cm).

The view of London looking east, shows the River Thames with the dome of St Paul's Cathedral and the spires of many London churches on the skyline. In the foreground is the old Strand Bridge which was re-named Waterloo Bridge after Wellington's victory at Waterloo two years before the bridge was opened in 1817. It was designed by George Dodd and built by John Rennie for a private company which raised over £1,000,000, recouping their expenditure by imposing tolls which were not abolished until 1878. Waterloo Bridge received high praise as one of the finest structures of its kind in Europe. Nine semi-elliptical arches supported a level roadway and pairs of Doric columns on the piers supported an entablature above which was a balustrade of grey granite from Aberdeen. The bridge was demolished in 1927 and the old shot tower on the south bank has also disappeared.

Vauxhall Gardens in London became a place of pleasure and amusement soon after 1660 in the reign of Charles II. An account in *Picture of London*, 1805, published a few years before the dish was made tells us that 'it was formerly little more than a tea-garden, enlivened with instrumental music; but its rural beauty and easy access rendered it so much frequented, that the proprietor was encouraged to speculate on public patronage. . . . Facing the west door is a large and superb orchestra, decorated with a profusion of lights in various colours. We are told that 5,000 to 15,000 well-dressed persons are occasionally present. The gardens open about the

Vauxhall Gardens, London
Dish (c. 1820–30) with a view of
the orchestra pavilion. Unmarked.
Width 9.4in (24cm).

middle of May and close about the end of August. The doors
are opened at seven o'clock and the concert begins at eight.'
The orchestral pavilion was a focal point in the Gardens and
greatly attracted Thomas Rowlandson, the artist. The
popularity of Vauxhall Gardens declined in the 1840s, despite
a reduction in the entrance fee, which brought in 'the rabble'.
They were closed in 1859 and were later sold by auction.

London : Villa in Regent's Park
Plate (c. 1830) in dark blue by
Adams (probably William Adams)
of Stoke-on-Trent. This view has
two people in the foreground and a
groom with horse and chaise near
the villa. Diameter 8.8in (22.4cm).

This villa was part of the 'town-planning' carried out by
John Nash (1752–1835) in his Regent's Park scheme.
    Some of the designs in the series of 'Views of London'
produced by Adams were after drawings by Thomas H.
Shepherd in *Metropolitan Improvements of London*, 1829,
others from engravings by J. Shury after drawings by West,
and some from drawings done by an artist by the name of
Cutts. The villa illustrated is from a Shepherd drawing and
was the residence of John Maberly. Adams used views of two

other villas in Regent's Park on their wares – the residence of the Marquis of Hertford, and the residence of G. B. Greenough.

There is little doubt that this series was made for export to America where they are frequently found. Indeed the firm used the American Eagle in their mark. The example illustrated, though recently purchased in London, is known to have come from America.

Lowther Castle, Westmorland
Indented dish attributed to Ralph Stevenson with acorn and oak leaf border. 19.2in × 14.9in (48.8cm × 37.8cm).

Lowther Castle, Westmorland, is near the village of Lowther and the grounds slope down to the wooded banks of the River Lowther. It lies about four miles south of Penrith. The building dates from 1802 and was built of light rose-coloured free-stone in the Gothic style. The castellated north front is 420 feet long with many turrets and there is a lofty embattled central tower. On the north side is a fine terrace 90 feet broad and 500 feet long.

Lowther Castle was the seat of the Earl of Lonsdale. Hugh Cecil Lowther, the fifth Earl (1857–1944) was a keen and popular sportsman, huntsman, boxer and yachtsman. The castle was demolished in 1957.

Lynmouth is a coastal village with a small harbour at the confluence of the East and West Lyn on the borders of Exmoor. It has always been regarded as one of Devon's beauty spots backed by vast woodland and moorland areas from which the river descends in a densely wooded gorge. In recent years this brought disaster to this little holiday town. On the night of 15 August 1952, when more than 6 inches of rain fell on Exmoor, the river broke its banks and flooded through the streets carrying all before it.

Why did the maker of this series of ceramic landscapes choose Lynmouth? It had already started to attract visitors even in the early nineteenth century. Robert Southey spoke

Lynmouth, North Devon
Moulded dish (c. 1820–40) by
unknown maker, clobbered
overglaze with coloured enamels,
and with gilded edge. Length
11.4in (29.2cm).

highly of its attractions and the poet Shelley stayed in
Lynmouth with his wife in 1812 and wrote some of his
revolutionary pamphlets. One was called 'A Declaration of
Rights' and this he is said to have put in bottles which he
floated out to sea. The authorities came to hear of this and
Shelley received word that he was about to be arrested and
bribed a fisherman to take him across the Bristol Channel to
Wales.

Menai Bridge, Anglesey
Central landscape from dish
(c. 1825–30) by Thomas Dimmock
(Junr) & Co. of Staffordshire.
Printed mark 'Select Sketches'
above a cartouche enclosing the
words 'Menai Bridge'. Below is
word 'Stoneware' and the initial
'D'. Diameter of printed landscape
5.2in (13.2cm).

The view of the Menai Bridge was adapted from the title
page of *Wales Illustrated in a Series of Views comprising the
Picturesque Scenery, Towns, Castles, Seats of the Nobility and
Gentry, Antiquities etc.* published by Jones & Co., Temple of
the Muses, Finsbury Square, London in 1830. The
engravings in this book were all based on drawings by Henry
Gastineau.

The design for the Menai Bridge across the Menai Strait was by Thomas Telford (1757–1834). It was constructed as a suspension bridge between 1819 and 1825. The roadway, 100 feet above high water, was suspended by four cables, each composed of four tiers of bars, so that in all there are 16 chains. The bridge was 570 yards long and had two carriage ways 4 yards wide, separated by a footpath 4 feet wide. To the right in the far distance the 112-foot column with a statue of the first Marquis of Anglesey, the hero of Waterloo, can be seen. No other 'Select Sketches' by Dimmock & Co. have been noted.

Newstead Abbey, Nottinghamshire Jug (c. 1830–35) in medium blue with floral border. Printed mark 'Newstead Abbey' and 'G.P.' (Glamorgan Pottery). Height 8.5in (21.6cm).

Newstead Abbey was at one time the residence of Lord Byron. When this jug was decorated the Great Hall of the Abbey had just been restored and was attracting some attention.

The jug was almost certainly made by the firm of Baker, Bevans & Irwin which operated the Glamorgan Pottery from 1813 to 1838.

Oxburgh Hall lies about seven miles south-west of Swaffham. Permission to build a fortified manor on the site was granted to Edmund Bedingfield by Edward IV and it was constructed of red brick in 1482 and remained in the Bedingfield family until it was given to the National Trust in 1952. A shallow moat was made around the manor which could be quickly flooded from the nearby river. The print on the tray shows a horse and rider crossing the bridge over the

View of Oxburgh Hall, Norfolk
Plate (c. 1810–15) with print
showing the old Great Hall.
Impressed mark 'Davenport'.
Diameter 8.1in (20.6cm).
(Some collectors consider this to be
Bisham Abbey.)

Oxburgh Hall, Norfolk
Comport tray, with pierced border
of oak leaves and acorns, attributed
to Ralph Stevenson. Unmarked.
The glaze shows a deep blue where
it has run against the foot rim.
Length 10.6in (27.9cm).

moat which leads to the most striking feature of the building,
a magnificent 80 feet high gatehouse tower with octagonal
turrets. The building was considerably changed in the
eighteenth century. The mediaeval hall and kitchen on the
south side were destroyed in the 1770s and extensions were
built to east and west. Some believe the view at the top of the
page to be the mediaeval hall before demolition.

Christ Church, Oxford
Indented plate (c. 1815–30) by J. &
W. Ridgway, with a college view
and figures in academic dress in the
foreground. Diameter 9.9in
(25.2cm).

Christ Church was the largest college in Oxford and the
college chapel is the cathedral of the city. The spire seen in
the print was built in the thirteenth century and rises to a
height of 144 feet. To the right, seen below the branch of the
tree is Tom Tower, built by Sir Christopher Wren in 1681.
Within the tower is the famous bell – 'Great Tom' – which
came originally from Osney Abbey.

This plate is one of an attractive series of Oxford and
Cambridge Colleges produced by J. & W. Ridgway of
Hanley, Staffordshire. All bear the same border with scrolled
medallions with two themes – children feeding a goat and
milking a goat.

Pains Hill is famous primarily for its gardens. They were
landscaped in the first half of the eighteenth century when the
land was bought by Charles Hamilton. He tried to reproduce
the landscapes seen in Old Master paintings, building temples
and creating ruins as necessary. The trees are particularly
fine, the cedars of Lebanon having grown to a great height.
Many visitors have lingered in these grounds including
Horace Walpole and Charles van Linné.

Mathew Arnold who lived nearby at Pains Hill Cottage
knew the gardens well and wrote of a canary called Matthias
he had given to his daughter:

> Here Matthias sang his fill
> Saw the gardens of Pains Hill;
> Here he poured his little soul,
> Heard the murmur of the Mole.

It was from the River Mole that the lake in Pains Hill gardens
was fed, using a water wheel.

Pains Hill, Surrey
Indented soup plate (c. 1822–41) in dark blue with a rural scene with horse-riders in parkland. Printed mark 'R. Hall's Select Views. Pains Hill, Surrey, Stone China'. Diameter 9.5in (24.1cm).

This plate uses the landscape as a miniature within a wide decorative border of fruit and flowers. William Adams also occasionally used this layout for his ceramic landscapes. These are invariably printed in the dark blue favoured for export wares for America.

Richmond Bridge, Surrey
Indented dish (c. 1825–35) by Pountney & Allies of Bristol with the characteristic border used by this partnership on all their wares with printed landscapes. Length 10.8in (27.5cm).

Richmond Bridge was built as a stone structure of five large arches which increase in height and span towards the central arch. The work was carried out between 1774 and 1777 using a design by James Paine (*c.* 1716–1789), the architect who also planned the stables and bridge at Chatsworth. Richmond and Twickenham were thus linked though tolls had to be paid at one of the elegant toll houses. These are well seen in an engraving by W. B. Cooke in *Views of Richmond and Vicinity*, 1837, reproduced by John Gloag in his book on *The English Tradition in Architecture*, 1963.

The design met with general approval. Thomas Maurice (1754–1824) who was for a time assistant keeper of manuscripts in the British Museum wrote the following poem on 'Richmond Bridge':

> Mark where yon beauteous bridge, with modest pride
> Throws its broad shadow o'er the subject tide;
> There Attic elegance and strength unite
> And fair proportion's charms the eye delight;
> There, graceful while the spacious arches bend,
> No useless glaring ornaments offend.

Pountney & Allies used several Thames-side views on their wares including a splendid view of Oxford with its colleges and a landscape with Park Place, Henley.

Stackpole Court, Pembrokeshire
A plate (1822–30) in medium blue, by Elkins & Co. The printed mark describes this as 'Irish Scenery'. Diameter 10in (25.4cm).

Stackpole Court was built in the eighteenth century in the parish of St Petrox, three miles south of Pembroke. Elkins & Co used several English landscapes in this series unaccountably called 'Irish Scenery', including one of Warwick Castle.

Stirling Castle, Stirlingshire
Indented dish (c. 1825–35). Printed
mark 'Antique Scenery' on
underside of rim. Combed base.
Length 13.2in (33.5cm). Width
10.4in (26.4cm).

Stirling Castle was built on the brow of a precipitous basalt
rock near to the River Forth. It has been involved in the
history of Scotland since Alexander I died there in 1124. In
1304 it held out for three months against Edward I at the head
of a powerful English army. So resolute was the defence that
besieging implements had to be brought from the Tower of
London, including a destructive engine called the Wolf. A
breach was made, the ditch was filled with stone and the castle
taken. Stirling remained in the possession of the English for
ten years. It was considered as such an important stronghold
that Edward II assembled a great army and undertook the
invasion of Scotland to prevent it falling into the hands of
Robert the Bruce, a campaign which ended in the defeat of
the English at Bannockburn. In the fifteenth century, it became
a royal residence for the Kings of Scotland. James II was born
in the castle, James III made considerable additions to the
building, James V was born and crowned at Stirling and
James VI was baptized within its walls. Mary, Queen of Scots,
who was born at Linlithgow Palace, was taken to Stirling
Castle when very young as a safer home, less likely to be
endangered by the English, and she lived here in the
Renaissance palace within the castle walls until she went to
France in 1548.

Taymouth Castle is about a mile from Kenmore on the
River Tay and near the foot of Loch Tay. When this view was
engraved it was the seat of the Earls of Breadalbane. This is
the finest of the country houses built by Archibald Elliot
(1761–1823) and James Elliot (d.1810) in castellated Gothic.
It was completed for the fourth Earl between 1806 and 1810.
Wings were added to the east and west by William Atkinson
between 1818 and 1828. The earlier part is a pile of four
storeys and round corner towers.
  The view of Taymouth Castle prompted Robert Burns to
write the following lines in which he refers to it as a 'palace':

Taymouth Castle, Perthshire
Plate (c. 1815–28) in dark blue by
J. & R. Riley of Burslem. Printed
mark 'Taymouth Castle,
Perthshire, Riley' on a ribbon
twined around a branch. Diameter
10in (25.4cm).

The meeting cliffs each deep-sunk glen divides,
The woods, wild scatter'd clothe their ample sides;
The outstretching lake, embosom'd 'mong the hills,
The eye with wonder and amazement fills;
The Tay, meandering sweet in infant pride;
The palace rising by its verdant side;
The lawns, wood-fringed, in nature's native taste;
The hillocks dropt in nature's careless haste;
The arches striding o'er the new born stream;
The village glittering in the moontide beam.

Burns was right, for the pleasure gardens of Taymouth Castle
were laid out with great taste.

Trentham Hall, Staffordshire
Plate (c. 1826–30) in medium blue,
attributed to C. J. Mason & Co.
Printed mark 'Semi-China
Warranted'. Diameter 10in
(25.4cm).

Trentham Hall in the parish of Trentham, Staffordshire,
the seat of the Duke of Sutherland, was on the banks of the
River Trent. The view on the plate shows the original

building in the Italian style which was considerably enlarged in 1838 under the direction of Sir Charles Barry (1795–1860) some years after the plate was made. Barry added a fine belvedere tower. Trentham Hall was dismantled in 1912; it is said that the water of the Trent was so badly polluted as to make life near it quite impossible.

Makers of Wares with blue-printed Landscapes

Adams
The Adams family of Staffordshire potters operated factories at Cobridge, Tunstall and Stoke-on-Trent over a considerable period. Most of the landscape scenes, however, were undoubtedly used by William Adams & Sons between 1815 and 1840. Many of these scenes were on wares exported to America. They are mainly dark blue in colour.

Bell
William Bell of the Belle Vue Pottery, Hull, Yorkshire, produced blue-printed wares with landscape patterns between c.1826 and 1841.

Careys
The name 'Careys' is frequently found on the pearlwares and stonewares of various Staffordshire partnerships between 1818 and 1842, mainly involving Thomas and John Carey. They operated the Anchor Works which was the only pottery to produce a landscape series of cathedrals. They also produced a series of 'Irish Views', which included such landscapes as 'Carrick Fergus Castle and Town'.

Clews
James and Ralph Clews produced many dinner services with landscape series between 1815 and 1834 and they had a considerable export trade to America. In 1837 James Clews started a pottery at Troy, Indiana but it failed mainly because of lack of proper clays.

Davenport
This Longport firm used a number of patterns showing country scenes.

Elkins
Marks with this name represent one of the many partnerships which include the name of Elkin – Elkin, Knight & Co., Elkin, Knight & Elkin, or Elkins & Co., which operated at Fenton or Lane End, Staffordshire between 1822 and 1830. The wares are seldom marked but the impressed marks have been noted in association with a 'rock cartouche' bearing the printed name of the landscape. Some of their landscape wares have a border very similar to a border used by Rogers.

Goodwins & Harris
The Crown Works, Lane End, Staffordshire, produced an interesting series known as 'Metropolitan Scenery' between 1831 and 1838. There is a fine view of Bow Bridge, for example. Their wares are seldom marked but a single piece has been recorded with the impressed mark of this firm and a Staffordshire knot. The series may well have been started by an earlier partnership in the 1820s for there were several changes of control before Harris joined the firm.

Hall
Ralph Hall of Swan Bank, Tunstall produced dark blue-printed landscape wares in large quantities from 1822 onwards almost entirely for the American market. They are seldom found by collectors in Britain.

Harvey
Charles Harvey and Sons of Longton, Staffordshire operated between 1818 and 1835 and produced a fine series of British scenes with a characteristic border. These carry a printed mark which names the locality on a scrolled ribbon but only very occasionally is the impressed mark 'Harvey' used.

Henshall & Co.
Henshall & Co. of Longport produced a series of 'British Views' in the 1820s with a fine fruit and flower border (see Little, W. L. *Staffordshire Blue*, 1969, plate 103).

Herculaneum Pottery
The finest wares from this Liverpool factory were produced before about 1830. The earlier scenes were of Indian subjects but a few English views appeared between 1820 and 1830. Subsequently, most of the printed wares were in black or sepia.

Mason
Only two landscapes are known which were used by the Mason family of Lane Delph and neither of them is named on the wares. William Mason used a view of an abbey (possibly Furness Abbey) between 1811 and 1824 and C. J. Mason & Co., a view of Trentham Hall on wares marked 'Semi-China, Warranteed', some of which were sold in Ireland through the Dublin firm of Higginbotham & Co.

Meir
John Meir & Son (*c.*1837–50) produced a series of about a dozen views under the title of 'Northern Scenery'. The landscapes are all Scottish, mainly of lochs and castles. They were taken from Thomas Beattie's *Scotland* published in 1838.

Mintons
Mintons produced a number of landscape patterns on miniature wares but no identifiable views have been found on

Miniature Minton plates and dishes printed in blue with the following views: (left to right) Abbey Mill, Lancashire; Lechlade Bridge; Tewkesbury Church; Donington Park, Leicestershire; Lanercost Priory; Kenilworth Priory. The dish with the Lanercost Abbey print is 5.8in (14cm) long.

normal tablewares. The miniatures carry a printed mark stating the locality, with the impressed mark MINTONS sometimes associated with a late year cipher (e.g. for 1915).

Phillips
George Phillips of Longport produced the well-known Eton College pattern. He operated a pottery at Longport between 1834 and 1848.

Pountney & Allies
This partnership operated the Temple Bank Pottery in Bristol and produced some very good quality printed wares including two series of landscapes. One series was of views around Bristol which included Chepstow Castle on the north side of the Bristol channel. There was also a series of views along the River Thames – Oxford; Park Place, Henley; and Richmond Bridge. The partnership lasted from 1816 to 1836 but the blue-printed wares were mainly produced in the last ten years and continued during the next partnership of Pountney & Goldney (1836–49).

J. & W. Ridgway
This partnership operated the Cauldon Place and Bell Works, Shelton, Hanley from about 1814 to 1830. Their most notable achievement in the blue-printed wares was the production of a series of views of Oxford and Cambridge Colleges.

J. & R. Riley
This Burslem firm produced a fine series of English landscapes between 1802 and 1828, mainly with country houses, all with a scrolled border.

John Rogers & Son
A fine series of landscape patterns was used by this Longport firm between 1814 and 1836 with a floral border. The view of Lancaster is a very good example. Although some examples bear the impressed mark 'Rogers', no known example carries a printed mark naming the view. A number of landscapes are therefore not identifiable.

Ralph Stevenson
Ralph Stevenson came from a family of Staffordshire potters and he operated the Lower Manufactory at Cobridge from about 1810 to 1832 though he may have been in partnership with Aldborough Lloyd Williams for a short period around 1825. The firm had a large export trade to America and used a fine oak-leaf and acorn border with many landscape patterns.

S. Tams & Co.
A few London views in dark blue were produced by this firm including The Royal Exchange, and Somerset House, and these probably date from *c.*1815 to *c.*1830 but there are no definite records available. During this period there were several partnerships one of which includes the name of Anderson.

Enoch Wood & Sons
This Burslem firm potted between 1818 and 1846 and concentrated on the American trade, though a number of English landscapes such as Cave Castle, Yorkshire, were produced in a fine dark blue.

Industrial and Urban Landscapes

Most of the blue-printed landscapes were of country houses, castles, abbeys or rural scenes with bridges. Very few industrial scenes were used. However, in the north-east of England, a number of potteries close to the River Wear were printing riverside scenes on their wares in black with shipping workers' cottages, pottery kilns and, in most cases, a bridge. The favourite scene was the Wearmouth Bridge which had been sponsored by Rowland Burdon MP (1756–1838) and which was opened on 9 August 1796. This was considered to be a remarkable engineering achievement. It was the largest single-span cast-iron bridge in the world and served the area for over sixty years when it was reconstructed following the advice of Robert Stevenson.

Twenty-six different prints of the original bridge have been recorded and five of the reconstructed bridge. (see Shaw, J. T. *The Potteries of Sunderland and District*, 1968). Most of

Wearmouth Bridge
Pink lustre jug (1813) by Dixon &
Co. of the Sunderland Pottery with
a view of the Wearmouth Bridge
printed in black. Height 7in
(17.8cm).

Shields : The Mouth of the Tyne
Pink lustre jug (1844) probably by
a Newcastle pottery with a black
print of the River Tyne. One panel
is hand-painted with the name
'Susan Bichard 1844' in a floral
cartouche. Unmarked. Height
8.7in (22.1cm).

these appear on jugs, mugs or bowls and they were made for
the gift trade. Many were taken by sailors to all parts of the
world. The black print was usually accompanied by a pink
lustre decoration with a speckled or mottled appearance, and
the wares carried verses and mottoes with a popular appeal.
The illustration (above, left) shows a typical example made by
Dixon & Co. at the Sunderland Pottery in 1813.

A more unusual industrial scene is printed in black with a
Tyneside scene. It shows the High Light and the Low Light
which guide the ships entering the river. A pottery kiln may
also be seen. A panel beneath the lip of the jug is hand-
painted with flowers and 'Susan Bichard 1844'. Bichard is a
Guernsey name and this is where the jug was found. It was no
doubt presented as a gift having been made specially for the
donor and almost certainly taken to the island on a collier. It
may well have been made in one of the Newcastle potteries,
possibly by Sewell & Donkin at St Anthony's Pottery.

After about 1830 the production of blue-printed wares with
landscapes was declining even in Staffordshire. There may
have been several reasons for this. The middle-class market
for dinner wares may well have become saturated and
attempts to produce wares more cheaply for the 'working
classes' meant that the expense of engraving a large number of
copper plates was precluded. Moreover, technical advances
made it possible to print in other colours – pink, green and
sepia. Whatever the reason, relatively few landscape prints
were used for many years. There were, of course, a few
exceptions.

In 1833 the Spode factory was taken over by William
Taylor Copeland who formed a partnership with Thomas
Garrett. The new firm of Copeland & Garrett produced
dinner services decorated with floral and geometrical motifs
on which a view of the Tower of London was printed in sepia.
The plate shows the landscape medallion in the centre of a
tureen stand.

The Tower of London from the Thames
Medallion printed in sepia in the centre of a tureen stand (1833–47) by Copeland & Garrett. An impressed mark includes the words 'Royal Opal'. The stand is 18in (45.7cm) long and the medallion print 3.7in (9.4cm) long.

The 'Royal Opal' presumably refers to one of the many bodies used by Copeland & Garrett; others included 'Stone China', 'Felspar Porcelain' and 'New Jasper Stone'.

Meanwhile, the Herculaneum Pottery, Toxteth, Liverpool was printing wares in black, sepia and blue with views of the city and the River Mersey taken from a book called *Lancashire Illustrated* published in London in 1832. A fine dish with a sepia print of Castle Street, Liverpool shows the Town Hall in the distance. It was adapted from an engraving by E. Wallis from a drawing by T. Harwood. The sepia print is a close copy of the original but a horseman, three ladies and a child have been added to the foreground to balance the picture. (See Smith, A. *Liverpool Herculaneum Pottery*, 1970.)

Castle Street, Liverpool
Meat dish (c. 1835) printed in sepia by the Herculaneum Pottery, Liverpool. Impressed Liver Bird mark. Length 20.5in (52.6cm). Courtesy Merseyside County Museums.

The Royal Exchange, London
Unattributed plate printed in sepia. Mark: An anchor surmounted by a crown within a wreath of leaves. Diameter 9.2in (23.5cm).

The Thames and St Paul's Cathedral
Gadrooned plate by Enoch Wood & Sons printed in sepia. Mark 'Celtic China. English Cities, London E. W. & S.'

Souvenir Wares and Special Orders

From about 1840 many potters printed wares for special occasions. An unknown potter produced a sepia view of the Royal Exchange which was opened by Queen Victoria in 1844. This was the third Royal Exchange building, the previous buildings having been destroyed by fire. The equestrian statue of the Duke of Wellington by Sir Francis Chantry was erected in front in his honour.

With the growth of the railways and the expansion of holiday resorts the souvenir trade grew apace. This is fully described in Ian T. Henderson's *Pictorial Souvenirs of Britain* (1974).

The sepia view of the Thames and St Paul's Cathedral by Enoch Wood & Sons may well have been designed to meet the demand for souvenirs which the many visitors to London could take home.

Wesley College, Sheffield
Large meat dish (c. 1850–70) probably by Davenport with underglaze sepia print of the college and grounds. Length 19in (48.3cm).

This period also produced 'special orders' printed with appropriate landscapes – toilet sets and dinner wares for hotels or institutions. This is a fine view of Wesley College in Sheffield, adapted from a print by J. & J. Parker of Sheffield, though the original print shows only nineteen boys and two masters in the grounds. The pathway has been made to curve round into the foreground and the five larger figures in the foreground are additions.

The building was designed by William Flockton of Sheffield and was completed on a site adjoining Glossop Road in 1840. It was originally known as the Sheffield Wesleyan Proprietory Grammar School. It started with 250 boarders who may have been children of missionaries abroad. As befits a Yorkshire school, cricket was obviously popular; several games in progress may be seen in the print. The staff, all wearing mortarboards, include at least one schoolmistress.

In 1905 it amalgamated with the Sheffield Royal Grammar School to become King Edward VII School which took over the former Wesley College in 1906. It is now (1980) the King Edward VII Comprehensive School but, unfortunately, the magnificent proportions of the building can no longer be appreciated since urban development has now obscured the view.

Chapter 2 Transfer-printed Landscapes of North America

British potters have found a ready market for their wares on American shores since before the American Revolution. Although the shapes, forms and patterns have changed during two hundred years of trade, landscapes have been one of the decorative themes which has found continual favour. This started with the great flood in the 1820 to 1840 period of what is now termed historical china: transfer printing of landscapes, buildings, historical events or personages. It continues today primarily in commemorative or souvenir scenes. Then, as now, most of these wares were transfer-printed and produced in Staffordshire.

The illustrations cover over one hundred years of earthenware manufacture from the dark blue prints of the 1820s, through the lighter colours of the 1830–40 period, with a few later examples of wares made in this country by Wedgwood and Royal Doulton.

A wide range of North America's geography is represented in the illustrations. In some cases the ceramic landscape is the only record left of a scene or building as it was in the early

Mitchell & Freeman's China and Glass Warehouse, Chatham Street, Boston
Plate (c. 1830) by William Adams of Stoke printed in dark blue. Diameter 10in (25.4cm). Courtesy Dr Faith Baver.

years of the nineteenth century. The landscapes illustrated have been described in some detail and background has been added to help make the ceramic scenes live. When known, credit is also given to the artist or engraver who created the scene transferred to the earthenware.

Although it took the British potter to make the wares, the American merchant was required to market the products. An example of this relationship is found by the representation of the Mitchell & Freeman's China and Glass Warehouse, Chatham Street, Boston on Staffordshire earthenware.

William Adams used this view between 1827 and 1832. The dates can be placed as Chatham Street was not named until 1827, while Mr Freeman had left the firm by 1832. The source of the view showing the china warehouse is unknown. However, the plate shows ships in the background at Long Wharf while men haul crates of earthenware into the warehouse. Imagine how many tons of earthenware must have passed through the building. It is the only historical view in dark blue made by William Adam and exemplifies the commercial activity of the early city of Boston.

John Hancock was a wealthy merchant, first Governor of Massachusetts, President of the Second Continental Congress and the signer of the Declaration of Independence who wrote in such a bold hand that King George would be able to read it 'without his specks'.

The Hancock house erected in 1737 stood at the edge of the

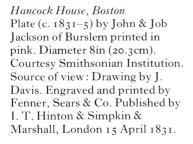

Hancock House, Boston
Plate (c. 1831–5) by John & Job Jackson of Burslem printed in pink. Diameter 8in (20.3cm). Courtesy Smithsonian Institution. Source of view: Drawing by J. Davis. Engraved and printed by Fenner, Sears & Co. Published by I. T. Hinton & Simpkin & Marshall, London 15 April 1831.

Boston Common to the left of the Boston State House. The view represented on the plate was drawn by J. Davis and published in London in 1831. The Staffordshire transfer in pink is by John and Job Jackson who were in business in Burslem from 1831 to 1835.

There is a charming anecdote concerning the hospitality of John Hancock in this house. The French Admiral d'Estaing during a visit in 1788 was invited for breakfast and arrived with so many of his officers that Mrs Hancock was obliged to send her servants out to borrow food from her neighbours and to milk the cows on the Common to feed the French entourage.

The house was offered to the State for preservation but the offer was rejected and the building was pulled down in 1863.

State House, Boston, 1818
Blue and white tile (1863–72) by Minton of Stoke. 6in × 6in (15.2cm × 15.2cm). Source of view: Sketch by Dobbins titled 'Boston Common in 1804'.

Harvard College
Plate (c. 1835) by Enoch Wood & Sons of Burslem, printed in light blue. Diameter 10.6in (26.9cm). Courtesy Smithsonian Institution. Source of view: Drawing by A. J. Davis. Engraved and printed by Fenner, Sears & Co. Published by I. T. Hinton & Simkin & Marshall, London 1 September 1830.

The State House, Boston designed by Charles Bulfinch was erected in 1795 on land previously owned by John Hancock. It faces Boston Common and is a most impressive early building with its columned façade and gilded dome.

The State House, Boston became one of the most popular American landscapes for British potters. Variations of two basic views were used by seven different potters during the period 1820–50. The illustrated blue and white tile was made by Mintons China Works, Stoke and carries that firm's mark for the period 1865–72. The front of the tile, based on a sketch by Dobbins, shows the title 'State House Boston 1818', while the reverse, besides the Minton mark states 'Published by Macullar Parker Company', a Boston concern of the late nineteenth century.

Harvard, located in Cambridge just outside of Boston, is the oldest higher education institution in the United States. It was founded in 1636 and named after John Harvard, a

Puritan Minister who contributed about 800 pounds and his library of some 300 volumes to the young college. The original purpose of the college was to train young men for the ministry. Religion was mixed with the classics and students were expected to speak only Latin in the college grounds.

Some 150 years later Harvard added University to its name, and its growth by the 1830s is reflected in the illustrated plate showing on the left Hollis Hall, Holworthy Hall and Holden Chapel, middle, Harvard Hall, and right, Stoughton Hall. All named as gifts from or memorials to these individuals.

Harvard was also well liked by the British potters for there are some dozen different views printed on earthenware by six Staffordshire potters.

Nahant Hotel near Boston
Plate (1828–30) by Stubbs & Kent of Burslem printed in dark blue. Diameter 8.8in (22.3cm). Courtesy Dr Faith Baver. Source of view: Drawing by J. R. Penniman. Engraved by Annin & Smith. Printed by Monroe & Francis. Published by Abel Bowen, Boston 1825.

This plate in a rich deep blue shows the characteristic eagle border used by the Burslem firm of Stubbs & Kent in the late 1820s. The Nahant Hotel was a resort hotel located a short distance from Boston and the following extracts from an advertisement in the *New York Commercial Advertiser* of 1 April 1824 best describe its features:

> This commodius and superior Hotel will be open for the reception of visitors on the first of May next ... it possesses advantages as a Summer Residence over any Watering Place on the Sea Coast of North America.

The stone edifice containing 70 chambers, dining room 50 feet in length to accommodate 125 persons at Table, plus Private Parlors.

Long and wide Plazzas surround the Hotel to shelter from heat of sun ... admirable promenade ... or place to rest for the lover of luxurious indolence.

Elevated upon a bed of Picturesque Rocks ... the moving scene of ships constantly passing ... the crossing of the ocean in a storm, and the tranquility of its bosom when the wind is silent ... uniting the beautiful and sublime.

Walks on the very borders of the sea, among the rocks, or over the smooth beach.

Plus Billiard Room, Bowling Alleys, Balls and Musical Parties and a Handsome Bathing House for warm and cold baths.

The subscribers flatter themselves that their Table will be abundently supplied ...

The Nahant Hotel was destroyed by fire in 1861, but certainly had been a popular resort for many years.

Nahant was an attractive resort during the early years of the last century, but after the Civil War the Boston intellectuals began to frequent Newport, Rhode Island. Later in the century that city reached its peak when the wealthy social set from New York also summered there in massive homes they built along the cliffs.

Newport's most enigmatic structure, however, is The Old Stone Mill. For a number of years it was claimed to be the remains of a visit by a Norseman in the eleventh century. It is now thought to be more probably the base of a seventeenth-century mill. This scene (above, left) was transferred to earthenware at the beginning of this century when there was a resurge of interest in historical scenes. Some original scenes were reissued in slightly different form, while many more scenes were added to the ceramic landscape.

One of the firms fostering this second wave of patriotism was Rowland & Marsellus Co., a New York importer. This plate carries their name and a fruit and flower border originally used by Ralph Hall of Tunstall in the 1820s on a series entitled 'Oriental Scenery'. It is not uncommon for new series to use material in this way from earlier work. Although the plate does not bear the mark of the British potter, statements by an employee of Rowland & Marsellus indicate it was mady by S. Hancock & Sons, who potted at Tunstall from 1858 to 1870 and then at Stoke until 1937.

It is not surprising to find that churches appear on Staffordshire wares made for a nation founded by people seeking religious freedom. The view of the two churches at Pittsfield, Mass. shows in the centre the large Congregational Church erected in 1793 by Charles Bulfinch; the smaller structure to the left and rear was the First Baptist Church built in 1827. The view therefore dates from the late 1820s.

This ceramic landscape by James and Ralph Clews is distinctive not only for repeating the church structure in the border, but for the fact that most pieces of a dinner service were made with the same view. Frequently on transfer ware, a view would only be used for plates of one size or a piece of holloware. The set was 'tied together' by the use of a common border. Here all pieces of the set used the same design.

The pastor of the Congregational Church during the Revolution was the Reverend Thomas Allen, an ardent patriot who served as Chaplain to the American Army under Washington. Folklore states that one Sunday morning he wore his Continental uniform under his gown, and during a zealous sermon, threw off his gown and led the male members of the church onto the Common, and under the elm tree depicted on the plate, formed the first detachment of the Berkshire Minutemen.

The city of New York with its church steeple skyline and busy harbour is shown in the view on the next page from Red Hook, with the Brooklyn Heights on the right of the platter.

It is based on a drawing made by William Guy Wall. Wall was a twenty-six year old Irish artist from Dublin when he arrived in New York on 1 September 1818. He met with an immediate success in America when people quickly recognised his technical perfection and the charm of his paintings. He produced many fresh and attractive landscape views of the United States in the early years of the last century.

The illustrated platter was one of the first two works of Wall which were transferred to Staffordshire wares. The other companion piece to it is titled 'New York from

Old Stone Mill, Newport, R. I. Plate attributed to S. Hancock & Sons, printed in dark blue. Diameter 10in (25.4cm). Courtesy Dave Arman. Source of view: Unknown.

Winter View of Pittsfield, Mass. Plate (c.1830) by James and Ralph Clews of Cobridge printed in dark blue. Diameter 6.5in (16.5cm). Courtesy Dr Faith Baver. Source of view: Unknown.

*New York from Heights near
Brooklyn*
Platter (1825–30) by Andrew
Stevenson of Cobridge printed in
dark blue. Diameter 16.2in
(41.2cm). Courtesy Smithsonian
Institution. Source of view:
Painting by W. G. Wall. Engraved
by J. Hill.

Weehawk', a view of the city from the New Jersey side.

Andrew Stevenson, the Staffordshire potter, was in New
York during the summer of 1823. It is probable that he saw
and admired these two views of New York and personally
contacted Wall at that time obtaining both views for use on
his Staffordshire wares.

Stevenson's efforts, moreover, started an association for
Wall which grew to include several other potters and many of
Wall's works appear on Staffordshire. Both James and Ralph
Clews, and their nephews, John and Job Jackson later each
made a series of views in lighter colours based on the works of
Wall.

*New York from Heights near
Brooklyn*
Print engraved by J. Hill from a
painting by William Guy Wall,
published in New York by
W. G. Wall, 1823. Courtesy New
York Historical Society

This is the print by William Guy Wall which Andrew
Stevenson transferred to the blue and white platter. The
availability of the print was first announced in the *New York
Commercial Advertiser* issue of 23 June 1823 in an
advertisement stating:

'Two aqua tints . . .
   New York from Weehawk
   New York from Heights near Brooklyn
to subscribers $12 – colored
ready mid August
Correct views of the City of New York,
have long been a desideratum, and it
has been a subject of surprise, that
no attempt has been made to exhibit to
the public the leading features of a
city, which possesses so great an
interest from its political and
commercial importance, as well as from
the natural beauties of the situation.
Original drawings . . . may be seen at
Mr. Hill, engraver, Hammond St. Greenwich.'

Records of James Hill, the engraver, preserved in the New York Historical Society show that he charged $150 for engraving the two plates (Brooklyn and Weehawk) and printed 500 impressions of each for $75.

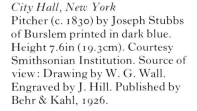

City Hall, New York
Pitcher (c. 1830) by Joseph Stubbs of Burslem printed in dark blue. Height 7.6in (19.3cm). Courtesy Smithsonian Institution. Source of view: Drawing by W. G. Wall. Engraved by J. Hill. Published by Behr & Kahl, 1926.

This is another example of Wall's work on Staffordshire. Although Andrew Stevenson also used this view for dark blue plates, this illustration is of a pitcher made by Joseph Stubbs in the late 1820s. The other side of the pitcher has a view of the State House, Boston. Perhaps views of the two major cities increased the marketing range and consumer appeal.

City Hall, built in 1811, is still standing and in daily use as the office of the Mayor. It has been called a mini-palace for a maxi-city. The building combines French Renaissance detail with Georgian form, probably because of the partnership of a French with a Scottish architect – Mangin and McComb. When built the building was located 'uptown' and faced toward New York at the foot of the island. It is now far downtown, but still preserves its commanding presence by the open spaces surrounding it.

American Museum
Plate (c. 1825) by Ralph Stevenson of Cobridge printed in dark blue. Diameter 7.5in (19.1cm). Courtesy Dr Faith Baver. Source of view: Unknown.

Castle Garden, Battery, New York
Platter (c. 1830) by Enoch Wood & Sons of Burslem printed in dark blue. Length 18.7in (46.5cm). Courtesy Smithsonian Institution. Source of view: Drawing by John Warner Barber.

The scene (above left) is the north end of City Hall Park, just behind New York's City Hall illustrated on the previous page. Today, New York seems to tear down good buildings to build something new, and probably higher. However, in earlier days, buildings were 'reused' for different purposes rather than being torn down. Such was the case with the building on this plate. It had been built as an almshouse in 1796 and used for that purpose for almost two decades. The scene *c.* 1822 depicted on the plate shows the American Museum occupying the west end of the building as the sign shows. This museum operated by John Scudders was a wonder of its day and one of its visitors reacted as follows:

> 'The object which most attracts our notice is a White Arctic Bear, in the highest preservation, a sight of which, alone, is worth more than the whole charge [a quarter of a dollar] of admission.'

After the departure of the American Museum to its own quarters in 1830, this building continued its functional life and was used for courts and offices under the name of 'The New City Hall'. It was destroyed by fire in 1854.

A New York building which has served a variety of uses is seen on a large platter (above right). It was built during the War of 1812 for harbour defence some 300 feet off the tip of lower Manhattan and Called Castle Clinton. By 1824 the structure had lost its military value and been renamed Castle Garden having been converted into a popular refreshment and entertainment spot featuring indoor gardens.

The most famous event associated with Castle Garden was the presentation of the Swedish soprano Jenny Lind on 11 September 1850 by P. T. Barnum, New York's famous showman of the day. Six thousand seats in the auditorium were sold out, and many more sat on the esplanade outside or in small boats in the harbour to witness the event. Jenny Lind received a sensational fee of $12,600 for her appearance, and promptly created another sensation by donating all her fee to philanthropic institutions.

Intervening years have seen land-fill entirely envelop Castle Garden while the structure continued its life as an immigration centre toward the end of the last century. For more than a quarter of this century it served as New York's aquarium, and, after much decay, is now restored as a fort and an historical monument.

Columbia College, New York
Plate (c. 1828–32) by Ralph Stevenson of Cobridge printed in dark blue. Diameter 7.5in (19.1cm). Courtesy Dr Faith Baver. Source of view: Drawing by A. J. Davis. Engraved by V. Balch. Printed by William D. Smith, December 6, 1828.

Burning of the Merchants' Exchange, New York
Plate (c. 1836) by an unknown potter printed in light blue. Diameter 10in (25.4cm). Courtesy Smithsonian Institution. Source of view: Lithograph by Alfred Hoffy. Printed and coloured by J. T. Bowen. Published for H. B. Robinson, NY January 1836.

Columbia College was originally called Kings College in honour of the charter granted by King George II on 31 October 1754. In 1784 the name was changed to Columbia College. Unlike its rival, Harvard, Columbia has always been a 'Middle of the city' school. The view on the plate is based on a drawing by A. J. Davis published in 1828. It shows the college building a few blocks from City Hall, New York, in the block bounded by Church Street, College Place, Barclay and Murray Streets.

The college was not as popular as Harvard, nor was it popular with the Staffordshire potters. Only this view was transferred to earthenware, although it was used both in the illustrated form by Ralph Stevenson and with a different border by his brother Andrew.

Above right is one of three views by an unknown potter to mark the New York fire of 16–17 December 1835. The other two views are 'Burning of New York from Coenties Slip' and 'Ruins of Merchants' Exchange'. Plates were printed in shades of black, light blue, pink, purple and sepia.

The Great Fire of New York started on the night of 16 December 1835 and burned all of the next day. By the time it was extinguished it had destroyed over 600 buildings south of Wall Street and the heart of the wholesale and merchant district of New York. Losses to buildings and the merchants' inventories was over 17 million dollars.

The Merchants' Exchange had been built of white marble less than ten years before the fire. The view on the light blue plate shows the firefighters' efforts, as well as salvaged material in the foreground, and fire equipment of the day is shown in the border.

Hudson River from Fishkill Platter (c. 1820) by James and Ralph Clews of Cobridge printed in light blue. Length 15.5in (39.4cm). Courtesy Smithsonian Institution. Source of view: Water-colour by W. G. Wall. Engraved by J. Hill. Published by Henry I. Megarcy, New York.

James and Ralph Clews produced a 'Hudson River' series which made use of a total of nineteen different views by W. G. Wall. This specific landscape was No.15 of Wall's 'Hudson River Portfolio' entitled *View of Fishkill looking to West Point*. The Clews brothers made a dinner set, tea set and toilet set in light shades of blue, pink, purple, sepia, black and brown using Wall's various drawings. The whole set was tied together by the common border of roses, birds and scrolls and records the early scenic landscapes of the Hudson Valley and River in about 1820.

West Point was a fort commanding an approach to the Hudson River during the Revolution. In 1788 a chain was stretched across the river at this point to stop the British from sailing up-river. The US Military Academy, the source of regular Army Officers, was founded at West Point by Act of Congress on 4 July 1802. Located some fifty miles north of New York City, it is today the oldest military post in the USA continually in use.

The view of West Point is one of the American views produced by William Adams & Sons in the 1830s in the lighter colours of pink, brown and black.

West Point Military School
Platter (c. 1830) by William Adams
& Sons of Stoke printed in pink.
Length 17.3in (43.9cm). Courtesy
Smithsonian Institution. Source of
view: Drawing by J. Milbert.
Engraved and printed by Fenner,
Sears & Co. Published by
I. T. Hinton & Simpkin &
Marshall, London 1831.

Harewood House, Yorkshire
Platter (c. 1825–30) by Ralph
Stevenson of Cobridge printed in
medium dark blue with
commemorative insets. Length
15in (38.1cm). Courtesy
Smithsonian Institution.

This platter is an early and rare example of the talent of the
British potter to combine several landscapes onto one ceramic
piece. The major scene shows Harewood House,
Yorkshire designed by Robert Adam and John Carr and
completed in 1771. The insets, however, turned it into an
early commemorative piece for the American market. It
combines two different memorable events: the return visit to
the United States by General Lafayette in 1824–25 and the
completion of the Erie Canal in 1825.

The medallion portraits are of two US Presidents: George
Washington and Thomas Jefferson, and the Governor of New
York State, DeWitt Clinton, who was instrumental in getting
the Erie Canal built. The other medallion states 'Welcome
Lafayette the Nation's Guest'. The Staffordshire potters

produced many different items of transfer ware to celebrate the return visit by the sixty-six year old Frenchman on his triumphal tour of his adopted land.

The Erie Canal inset at the bottom of the platter shows 'Entrance of the Canal into the Hudson at Albany'. The canal was opened on 26 October 1825 providing westward expansion of commerce through the 363-mile canal which linked the Hudson River, and thus the sea, with the inland Great Lakes. The Canal took eight years to build and cost over 7 million dollars. The Erie Canal inset was never used by Ralph Stevenson as a landscape by itself, but was used on pieces of transfer ware attributed to Enoch Wood & Sons.

Dutch Church at Albany
Pitcher (c. 1825) by Andrew Stevenson of Cobridge printed in dark blue. Height 8in (20.3cm). Courtesy Smithsonian Institution. Source of view: Lithograph drawn by P. Hooker. Engraved by Snyder. Published by John Low, New York 1806.

The printing on the pitcher describes it as a view of the late Protestant Dutch Church in the City of Albany, erected in 1715 and pulled down in 1806. This was the third Dutch Church of Albany, the first being built in 1642. The pitcher is important since it has preserved a view of the earliest type of church building in America. It is also a reminder of the early ties of Holland and America.

Andrew Stevenson and his brother Ralph Stevenson sometimes cause confusion. Both were potters in Cobridge over much of the same period of time during the early part of the last century. Both catered for the American market. However, they never potted together. This piece is marked 'Stevensons Stone China', which might add additional confusion but, fortunately, other pieces are known which carry this mark as well as the impressed circular 'A. Stevenson Warranted Staffordshire'. This pitcher was made by Andrew. The floral and cellular background is also sometimes found on wares of J. & R. Clews.

Niagara Falls from the American Side
Platter (c. 1830) by Enoch Wood & Sons of Burslem printed in dark blue. Length 14.8in (37.6cm). Courtesy Smithsonian Institution. Source of view: Sketch by J. Milbert. Engraved by Deroy. Published by H. Gaugain, France 1828.

Niagara Falls was first noted by the French explorer LaSalle in 1678. It has been a popular spot for travellers ever since. The falls are a part of the border between Canada and the United States where the Niagara River spills over a 165-foot precipice to create spectacular waterfalls. The view is from an engraving by Deroy published in France in 1828. It shows the American side of the falls with Goat Island in the middle of the dark blue platter.

Montreal
Platter (c. 1835) by W. Davenport & Co. of Longport printed in medium brown. Length 17in (43.2cm). Courtesy Smithsonian Institution. Source of view: Drawing by R. A. Sproule. Engraving by W. Leney. Published by A. Bourne, Montreal 1830.

The British potters made wares with scenes to appeal to the Canadian market such as this landscape produced by William Davenport & Co. in the 1830s showing Montreal from St Helen's Island. The view is found in medium shaded colours of pink, brown and blue. The scene features the steamship *British America* which was built in 1829 and plied the St Lawrence River from Montreal to Quebec until almost mid-century.

W. Davenport & Co. did not produce any historical views of the United States, but did make transfer ware with other types of decoration destined for both North American markets.

Heights of Quebec
Vegetable dish (c. 1825) by Enoch Wood & Sons of Burslem printed in dark blue. Width 9.5in (24.1cm). Courtesy Smithsonian Institution. Source of view: Unknown.

Fall of Montmorenci near Quebec
Plate (c. 1825) by Enoch Wood & Sons of Burslem printed in dark blue. Diameter 9in (22.9cm). Courtesy Dr Faith Baver. Source of view: Unknown.

Champlain started a French colony in Quebec in 1608. The English and the French fought over the city until 1759 when the British gained possession, although the French influence is still very strong. It is a picturesque city with its 'Upper Town' on the heights above the St Lawrence River, and its 'Lower Town' containing the commerce and harbour areas.

Views of Quebec were printed on ceramics by several potters, but the source of the view used for the dark blue vegetable dish is unknown. The cover for this dish has four different views on its four sides, all views of the United States. In the 1820s when this dish was made the Staffordshire potters probably thought of North America as one market.

The most interesting feature of the landscape (above right) is the 'house' on the left side of the falls. Although the unknown artist may have taken some liberties in the rendering of the size and exact location of the 'house', it did exist. It was built by Sir Frederick Haldimund, the British Governor-in-Chief of Canada in about 1780. The wife of the Lt Gen. John Graves Simcoe describes in her diary a visit made in 1782:

'the General begged my hand to show me into a small house, which was, as it were suspended on the cataract ... the foundations of the house consisted of eight strong beams laid athwart, beneath which the cataract hurried down with tremendous velocity'.

But the beams rotted and the house disappeared, although the falls remained a popular tourist attraction.

A View of the Residence of the late Richard Jordan taken from Newtown Meeting House, New Jersey
Print, drawn by W. Mason, engraved by F. Kearney. Courtesy Gary Stradling.

The Residence of the late Richard Jordan, New Jersey
Plate (1828–41) by J. Heath & Co. of Tunstall printed in mulberry. Diameter 10in (25.4cm). Courtesy Dr Faith Baver. Source of view: Unknown.

Richard Jordan was a Quaker Minister who lived and preached at Newtown, New Jersey, across the Delaware River from Philadelphia, from 1809 until his death in 1825. In his youth in Norfolk, Va. he took up the ministry after being cut off from his inheritance over the issue of slavery by his slave-owning father. He became an eminent preacher of the Friends, first at Hartford, Conn., and then at Newtown, New Jersey.

After his death friends commissioned W. Mason, a Philadelphia drawing teacher to sketch his house, including a figure thought to depict the man himself in the lane in front of the residence. The illustration shows this drawing as engraved by F. Kearny.

A footnote in a history of Gloucester County, New Jersey, published in 1845, explains the print coming to be on earthenware (though hopefully with more accuracy than as to where it was made):

'The Jordan residence is still standing ... an excellent drawing of it was made by Mr Mason. This was engraved and afterwards sent to China, where it was copied upon tea-setts, and other articles of chinaware. The picture may now be met with at public table, in barber shops, and in the crockery stores from one end of the Union to the other.'

Not only were 'tea-setts' made, but all articles of a dinner service, plus a pitcher and washbowl of a toilet set. It is found in black, medium blue, brown, lavender, maroon, mulberry, pink and purple. The mark is generally a printed umbrella with the name of the scene below and the initials 'J. H. & Co.'. A few pieces have been found with the entire maker's name shown, so it is with certainty that it was made by Joseph Heath & Co. in business from 1828 to 1841 in Tunstall. It is the only American scene produced on transfer ware by that firm.

Contrast the print features with those of the view of the plate. Note how the British potter has added a tree to 'fill in' the area on the left side, but with that exception how faithful the pottery reproduction is to the print, thus showing the full historic value of ceramic representation.

Pennsylvania Hospital, Philadelphia
Platter (1820–30) by J. & W. Ridgway of Hanley printed in dark blue. Length 18.5in (47cm). Courtesy Dr Faith Baver. Source of view: Drawing by George I. Parkyns. Engraved by W. Cook, London 1802.

Philadelphia Library
Plate (1820–30) by J. & W. Ridgway of Hanley printed in dark blue. Diameter 8in (20.3cm). Courtesy Dr Faith Baver. Source of view: Drawing and engraving by William Birch & Son. Published by R. Campbell & Co., Philadelphia 1799.

J. & W. Ridgway produced only one series with American views, their 'Beauties of America'. It consists of twenty-two different views of government, public business, religious or medical buildings. The medallion border of rose and leaf unite the various pieces of the dark blue dinner service.

This long platter is the next to largest piece of the series. It shows the Pennsylvania Hospital, the oldest in the nation, as it looked during the first decade of the 1800s. The hospital which was founded by the efforts of Ben Franklin remains today on the original location in Philadelphia between 8th and 9th Streets, and Pine and Spruce Streets.

Besides the hospital, Franklin was instrumental in starting the first circulating library in the United States. The library was the outgrowth of the Juno Club, located in a room of Robert Grace's home, where gentlemen of Philadelphia had deposited their personal books, and from which any civil gentlemen who cared to might borrow books to carry home 'into the bosom of private families'.

The first separate library building, shown on the J. & W. Ridgway plate, carries these words on its cornerstone laid in 1789:

At the instance of Benjamin Franklin,
Instituted the Philadelphia Library;
Which though small at first,
It became highly valuable and extensively useful;
And which the walls of this edifice
Are now destined to contain and preserve.

A statue of Franklin in a Roman toga can also be seen over the doorway carved in Italian marble. Inside, the circulating library had a request box which showed a head of a lion with an open mouth and this statement:

Gentlemen are requested to deposit
in the Lion's mouth the titles of
such books as they wish to have imported.

Bank of the United States, Philadelphia
Plate (1822–35) by Joseph Stubbs of Burslem printed in dark blue. Diameter 10in (25.4cm). Courtesy Dr Faith Baver. Source of view: Drawn and engraved by W. Birch & Son. Published by W. Birch, 31 December 1800, Philadelphia.

United States Hotel, Philadelphia
Soup plate (c. 1830) by S. Tams & Co. of Longton printed in dark blue. Diameter 10in (25.4cm). Courtesy Dr Faith Baver. Source of view: Drawing by G. Strickland. Engraved by F. Kearney. Published by Benjamin Renslow.

Built in 1795 as the Bank of the United States when Philadelphia was the Capital, Congress refused to renew its charter when it expired, so in 1812 Stephen Girard purchased the building for his own bank. Stephen Girard had almost as much influence on Philadelphia's development during the early part of the 1800s as Franklin had had a generation before. The bank became known as Girards National Bank, by which name it continues to this day.

When built, this was the most lavishly adorned building in the Quaker city with its stately marble portice and Corinthian columns. The old houses at the side of the bank add interesting detail of the style of the period.

The view on this plate was drawn, engraved and published in Philadelphia by William Birch. He and his son, Thomas, were both skilled painters and engravers. They were born in Warwickshire, England but settled in Philadelphia in 1794. He produced many views of his new nation, of which this one comes from his 'Views of Philadelphia', 1798–1800.

The United States Hotel opened on Chestnut Street in Philadelphia in 1826 and operated for some thirty years. The hotel was famous for its fashionable 'Assemblies' where every Thursday evening during the season, precisely at six o'clock, the fashionable of Philadelphia would gather to dance and play cards.

The United States Hotel was the subject for the little-known firm of S. Tams & Co. It is found on 10 in soup plates and 10 in dinner plates and has a depth effect created by the light clear background of the hotel set off by the dark blue of the deep foliage border, seen in the previous illustration.

The Longton firm may have been related to the Philadelphia crockery-importing firm of James Tams, in business from 1818 to 1840. These plates might have been a special order placed by the American merchant end of the family to be produced by the British potting arm of the family.

Upper Ferry Bridge over the River Schuylkill
Platter (c. 1830) by J. Stubbs of Burslem printed in dark blue. Length 18.8in (47.8cm). Courtesy Dr Faith Baver. Source of view: Drawing by T. Birch. Engraved by Jacob Plocher.

Dam and Water Works, Philadelphia
Plate (1825) by Henshall & Co. of Longport printed in dark blue. Diameter 10in (25.4cm). Courtesy Dr Faith Baver. Source of view: Drawing by T. Birch. Engraved by R. Campbell. Published by Edward Parker, 1824.

This platter shows two distinctive features of early American landscapes: the covered bridge and the covered wagon, and is based on a drawing by Thomas Birch.

This original design for a covered bridge produced the longest wooden single-span bridge in the United States when built in Philadelphia in 1812. It was officially called Upper Ferry Bridge but the 340-foot span quickly became known as 'The Colossus' and certainly seems worthy of that nickname. It was designed by Louis Wernwag and spanned the Schuyl-kill at Spring Garden Street until destroyed by fire in 1838.

In the foreground of the platter is a Conestoga wagon, the covered wagon designed and built in Pennsylvania which was the major vehicle of America for over a hundred years from 1750 to 1850. It was not only used for westward migration, but in the east for freight before being replaced by the railroads in the middle of the nineteenth century. The Conestoga wagon is marked by the gently curved slightly higher front and back ends. The reason the United States drives on the right-hand side of the road (unlike the British) is attributed to the Conestoga wagon. The wagoner drove from the left side, seated or standing on the lazy board. Later vehicles retained the left side as the proper position for the driver.

Besides 'The Colossus' another attraction of the Schuylkill was the Dam and Water Works for pumping water into a reservoir in Fairmount Park. This view, again based on a drawing by Thomas Birch, shows an example of beneficial city planning by early Philadelphia. The blending of several purposes in harmony was described in its day as being 'a glory of Philadelphia, combining beauty of scenery, usefulness of purpose and magnitude of design'. Would that city planners do so well today!

In the early 1800s, Faire Mount, as it was originally called, or Fairmount Park as it is known today, was a popular spot of nature for Philadelphians to bring the family to enjoy air, trees and grass. Here we see the Doric building erected in 1813 housing the water works and offices, with the dam in the right foreground holding the reservoir.

Two examples of this view are attributed to Henshall for reasons given later. The scenes were the same except for the boats; one view has a stern wheeler (shown), while the other has a side-wheeler craft in the similar place. Both were powered by steam and went at a 'fast rate of steam' to judge by the white wave lines alongside and aft of the craft.

Court House, Baltimore
Plate (c. 1835) attributed to Henshall & Co. of Longport printed in medium blue. Diameter 8.5in (21.6cm). Courtesy Dr Faith Baver. Source of view: Engraving from 'Picture of Baltimore, Maryland' published by Fielding Lucas, Jr 1832. Printed by A. T. Francis.

Holliday Street Theatre, Baltimore
Cup plate (c. 1835) attributed to Henshall & Co. of Longport printed in dark blue. Diameter 3.5in (8.9cm). Courtesy Dr Faith Baver. Source of view: Engravings from 'Picture of Baltimore, Maryland' published by Fielding Lucas, Jr 1832. Printed by A. T. Francis.

Several of the views of Baltimore found on Staffordshire ware were for many years classified as 'maker unknown'. Such was the situation of these two views. However, in 1969, W. L. Little in his *Staffordshire Blue* mentions an English view with the same fruit and flower border found with the name Henshall & Co impressed on the reverse. As Staffordshire potters generally did not pirate each others borders, it is now considered that S. Henshall & Co. of

Longport was the maker of these two illustrated views of Baltimore, as well as the view of Philadelphia's Water Works.

The view of the 8.5 in diameter plate on the previous page shows the Baltimore Court House in a brilliant medium dark blue. The Court house was built in 1808 at Lexington Street and Monument Square and had an imposing 145-foot frontage. The second view is of a 3.5 in cup plate of the Holliday Street Theatre, Baltimore, built in 1813 by Robert Carey Long. The view is only known on the small cup plate, a piece of Staffordshire transfer ware made for the overseas market which is not known in England. Much discussion continues on the use and origin of the cup plate. It would appear to be an American vogue started with glass cup plates, but quickly adopted and supplied to the American market by the English potters during the first quarter of the last century.

Capitol at Washington
Platter (1825–30) by J. & W. Ridgway of Hanley printed in dark blue. Length 20.5in (52cm). Courtesy Smithsonian Institution. Source of view: Drawing by H. Brown, engraved and printed by Fenner, Sears & Co. Published by I. T. Hinton & Simpkins & Marshall, London March 15, 1831.

The US Capitol was the centre-point of the design for the city of Washington created by the Frenchman, Major L'Enfant at the end of the eighteenth century. It was placed upon the summit of a hill with roads radiating from it. The building was started in 1793 from designs of William Thornton. It had all but been completed when the British attacked Washington and burned the Capitol, and most of the city, in August 1814. The rebuilding was slow, but with sophisticated refinements added by Charles Bulfinch, the man who designed the State House, Boston. When Lafayette paid his return visit to the nation in 1824, workmen were still busy with construction.

Although the British may have destroyed the city, they recognized the glory of it also, for no less than six Staffordshire potters used transfer designs of the city.

The illustrated view shows the US Capitol before the great dome had been added. It is the largest piece of Ridgway's 'Beauties of America' series.

President's House, Washington
Plate (c. 1830) by Enoch Wood &
Sons of Burslem printed in light
blue. Diameter 10.5in (26.7cm).
Courtesy Dr Faith Baver. Source
of view: Drawing by H. Bowen.
Engraved and printed by Fenner,
Sears & Co. Published by
I.T. Hinton & Simpkin &
Marshall, London February 15,
1831.

Washington Mansion, Mt Vernon
Plate (early twentieth century) by
Royal Doulton of Burslem in
medium blue. Diameter 9.8in
(24.9cm). Source of view:
Unknown.

The President's House, Washington (left), as originally
known, was started in 1793. Although still uncompleted, it
became the home of President Adams when he and the US
Congress formally moved from Philadelphia to the new
capital city during the fall of 1800. The story of Abigail
Adams's use for the East Room is still told with delight: to
dry the family laundry!

The house finally reached the liveable stage some fourteen
years later when Dolly Madison was forced to flee from the
British at very short notice, but not before she made sure that
the portrait of George Washington left with her. The
President's House, and all its contents, were burned by the
British Army in August 1814.

Actually, it is because of that burning of the mansion by the
British that it is now known as the White House. To cover the
scars of the fire, the exterior was painted white, and the name
stuck and is now the official name of the President's House.
The view on the platter is from the reconstructed period of
the late 1820s or early 1830s.

Although George Washington did not live to see the US
Congress move to the city named after him, he was largely
responsible for its design and location. Washington, DC is
some fifteen miles north of Mount Vernon, the ancestral
home of the Washington family.

The original mansion was built in 1743 by George
Washington's brother, Lawrence, and named after a British
family friend, Admiral Edward Vernon. Located on a bluff
overlooking the Potomac River, George Washington lived
here and expanded the home to the two-and-a-half-storey
wooden building with its colonnade and piazza as shown
(above right). This photographic likeness was made by Royal

Doulton early this century for G. H. Bowman Co., who were in business from 1888 to 1932. Besides the Royal Doulton mark, the reverse of the plate also has the mark of the customer: 'The George H. Bowman Co. Sole Importers Cleveland'.

Exchange, Charleston
Tray (c. 1825) by J. & W. Ridgway of Hanley printed in dark blue. 8.3in × 5.5in (21.6cm × 14cm). Courtesy Dr Faith Baver. Source of view: Drawing by Joshua Shaw. Engraved by W. G. Mason, Published by I. C. Kayser & Co. 1823.

The Charleston Exchange was built in 1767 at the east end of Broad Street near the Cooper River. In 1818 the building was sold to the US Government who used it as a customs house and then port office. This century the building returned to the State and is an historical monument.

This building is in the city associated with the spark which set off the Civil War. South Carolina had formally seceded from the Union in December 1860 after the election victory of Lincoln, and was one of the seven states which created the Confederate States of America in February 1861. However, war did not actually break out until the Confederate batteries opened fire on the Federal troops in Fort Sumter in Charleston harbour in April 1861, setting off the bitter Civil War.

The washbowl opposite (left) shows one of four scenes in lighter colours by Ralph Stevenson from sketches made by Captain Basil Hall, RN, and published by him in his *Forty Etchings from Sketches made with the Camera Lucida in North America in 1827–1828*. Captain Hall's comments concerning Riceborough and the view shown on the washbowl are:

> The villages in the State of Georgia, especially on the sea coast, are most of them very pretty. The building here represented is what is called a frame house, being made of timber squared and fastened together, and afterward covered with planks at the ends and sides.... Almost all the houses in that part of the country have verandahs, or what they call piazzas.

Riceborough, Georgia
Washbowl (c. 1830) by Ralph
Stevenson of Cobridge printed in
black. Diameter 12in (30.5cm).
Courtesy: Smithsonian
Institution. Source of view:
Drawing by Captain Basil Hall,
R. N. Engraved by W. H. Lizards.
Published by Cadell & Co.
Edinburgh 1829.

Mormon Temple, Nauvoo, Illinois
Plate (c. 1845) by Joseph Twigg of
Swinton printed in medium blue.
Diameter 9.3in (23.6cm).
Courtesy Smithsonian
Institution. Source of view:
Unknown.

A rare piece of transfer ware (above right) shows the Temple
which the Mormons erected in Nauvoo, Illinois during
1841–1846. The inscription reads: The House of the Lord
built by the Church of Jesus Christ of Latter-day Saints.
Commenced April 6 AD 1841. Holiness to the Lord.

The Mormons, as the group has always popularly been
called, were driven out of Missouri in 1839 and settled in
Illinois on the banks of the Mississippi River in a town they
renamed Nauvoo. But the stay of the Mormons here was to be
short and not peaceful. The murder of their founder and
leader Joseph Smith, difficulties over polygamy and other
troubles culminated in what was called the Second Mormon
War. In the fall of 1845, Brigham Young, their new leader,
bid for time by promising to take his followers out of Illinois
'as soon as grass grows and water runs'. He did not get his
prayer in full, for the first group started the exodus in
February 1846 and, under much pressure, the whole colony
of over 14,000 had left Nauvoo by late summer 1846. The trek
was westward and was to end in the founding of their new
Zion a year later at what is now Salt Lake City, Utah.

The medium blue plate has the names of the twelve
Apostles of the Church around the border. It was made by the
Yorkshire potter Joseph Twigg in the 1840s. It is the only
piece of transfer ware for the American market known to have
been made by this firm and may have been a special order
placed by one of the Mormon church members whilst
preaching in England.

Louisville, on the Ohio River, prospered with the advent of
the steamboat on the Mississippi and Ohio Rivers during the
late 1810s. This 1820s view shows Sixth Street of Louisville
running down to the river, and the extensive river traffic.

The steamboat permitted Louisville firms to import goods
from England through New Orleans. Records of a Louisville

Louisville, Kentucky
Vegetable dish (c. 1825) by James and Ralph Clews of Cobridge, printed in dark blue. Length 11.8in (30cm). Courtesy Smithsonian Institution. Source of view: Unknown.

Marine Hospital, Louisville
Plate (c. 1825) by Enoch Wood & Sons of Burslem printed in dark blue. Diameter 9in (22.9cm). Courtesy Dr Faith Baver. Source of view: Unknown.

earthenware import firm from 1833 show transfer-ware plates sold for 10 cents each, wholesale. That most inexpensive price covered not only the making of the plate, the shipping of it down the Mersey Canal, ocean crossing from Liverpool to New Orleans, transhipment over 1,000 miles up river, insurance, but a profit for both the manufacturer in England and the merchant in the mid-west of America.

The vegetable dish is now considered to have been made by James and Ralph Clews, although it does not bear a mark. After that firm went bankrupt in Cobridge in November 1834, James Clews and his family emigrated to Louisville to attempt to produce similar wares there. The undertaking was coordinated by Samuel Casseday, a Louisville merchant, and opened in January 1837 as the Indiana Pottery Co., some fifty miles downriver from Louisville on the other side of the river at Troy, Indiana. James Clews was a part of the management of the pioneer American concern for five years until the spring of 1842, but then eventually returned to Hilderstone, near Stoke by 1849. He died there on 13 July 1861 at the age of seventy-one, with a manufacturing career spanning two continents.

The steamboat not only brought commerce up and down the Mississippi and Ohio Rivers, but hazards as well. To the reader of Mark Twain, the appeal of the river, its people and its steamboats is well known. Steamboat wrecks were frequent, not only due to the shifting currents, sand bars and changing water levels, but also due to the tendency of riverboat captains to race one another, sometimes to the point where the craft literally blew up when the boilers were asked for too much steam.

The sobering influence of these hazards is shown in this view of the Marine Hospital built in Louisville in 1820 by the government to care for sailors who became injured or sick working on the Mississippi or Ohio Rivers.

Although the Marine Hospital is gone, its site is now occupied by the Louisville General Hospital.

Chapter 3   A Wedgwood Postscript

One very famous pottery did not compete in the early nineteenth-century export trade in printed wares – Josiah Wedgwood's Etruria. In the last quarter of the century, however, Wedgwood established a flourishing trade in blue-printed wares with North America. It started with a souvenir pitcher made in 1876 for the US Centennial Fair in Philadelphia with views of the Fair printed in black. This marked Wedgwood's entry into the American landscape field which was to grow rapidly over the years.

Five years later a strong link was forged between Wedgwood and the Boston china importers – Jones, McDuffee & Stratton, a relationship which started in 1881 and continued for almost three-quarters of a century. The year 1881 is firmly established for it was the first year in which a distinctive ceramic tile calendar was produced. This tile had the year calendar printed on one side and an American view on the other, generally a view of New England with some historical significance. In 1910, some 12,000 calendar tiles were produced to be given away to the firm's clients, a practice which lasted some fifty years. This gives some idea of the firm's size.

King's Chapel and *Boston Light*
Ceramic tiles with calendars for 1898 and 1916 respectively. Such tiles had an historical view on one side and the calendar on the other. 4in × 5in (8.2cm × 10.7cm).

The calendar tiles proved so popular that a series of blue transfer-printed plates was produced which Jones, McDuffee & Stratton termed 'Wedgwood Old Blue Historical Plates'. These plates have a distinctive border of flowers and foliage and the centre of the plates carried views of the United States which the importers stated 'were engraved for us by Josiah Wedgwood & Sons from famous paintings and picturesque etchings of historical interest to all Americans'. The sales brochures and advertisements stated that the plates were 'equally adapted to decorative purposes and table service.

United States Capitol
Blue and white transfer-printed
plate. The reverse side states that it
was 'Made by Wedgwood for
Jones, McDuffee & Stratton Co.'
Copyright 1900. Diameter 9in
(22.9cm).

*The Library of the School of
Business Administration, Harvard*
A blue-printed view, one of a
dozen different views in a series
produced for Harvard in 1927.
Diameter 10.5in (26.7cm).

The subjects are excellent for the plate rail effect'. The plate rail was a moulding on the walls of the dining room for displaying plates and with the size of rooms at the turn of the century one can well understand that Jones, McDuffee & Stratton were opening up an enormous market.

The first series of blue historical plates was issued in 1899 when 35 different views were covered by copyright; by 1910, 78 different views were on offer and eventually well over 100 landscapes were produced, all tied together with the distinctive flower and foliage border.

In the 1920s the Boston importers sponsored another Wedgwood enterprise— series of plates with views of schools, colleges and other educational institutions. Some series had only two different views; others ran to a full dozen. The leader of the pack was Harvard University for whom four series were produced with 48 views in all. Eventually over 100 different series were issued showing educational establishments, often with distinctive borders.

Most of the wares with American views produced by Wedgwood bear the trade mark of Jones, McDuffee & Stratton, though some also have the name of the retail store which sold them. There was, however, one other importer of chinaware who established close ties with Wedgwood – Van Heusen, Charles of Albany, New York. This firm had been the American agent for the production of a set of Presidential China for Theodore Roosevelt in 1904. The service did not feature landscapes, simply the Great Seal of the United States on each article. It was the only service ever produced by Wedgwood for an American President. After such an order it was understandable that Van Heusen, Charles were able to deal directly with Wedgwood for landscape wares though the only series ordered consisted of twelve different blue-printed views of Albany and its environs with borders of bluebells and foliage.

The importers in Boston and Albany had provided the entry for Wedgwood into the American market. By 1906 Wedgwood had established its own office in New York under the direction of Kennard Wedgwood. Business expanded and by 1920 Wedgwood had established an American subsidiary to handle the US business directly, an arrangement which continues today. Many items produced for export to America do not find their way on to the British home market though they sometimes turn up as souvenirs brought back by travellers.

Since 1950 Wedgwood has produced exclusive American landscape series for large department or speciality stores including the following:

Scenes of Old New York	B. Altman & Co, NY
Philadelphia Series	John Wanamaker's
Federal City Series	Charles Schwartz, DC
Atlanta Series	Rich's, Inc.
Historic Boston Series	H. Stearns Co.
Chicago Series	Marshall Field & Co.

The first British views produced by Wedgwood at this period for the home market were to celebrate their own 200th anniversary in 1959. The items showed views of Barlaston, Etruria, etc. as well as views of Josiah Wedgwood's birthplace and his first pottery. That initial entry into the domestic landscape market was followed by several plates in limited editions and by Christmas plates and mugs, all with British views. There had been a series of views of London produced in the 1940s but that was for the British War Relief organisation in the USA and Canada as a fund-raising project.

In 1969 came a new departure – the production of Christmas plates in jasperware, probably the most famous of the ceramic wares invented by Josiah Wedgwood. The ware had been used for classical themes since 1774 and has been in continual production since that time but never before for an English landscape. The 1969 plate had a view of Windsor Castle in relief and is now difficult to find. In the following years the plates included views of London – Trafalgar Square, Piccadilly Circus, St Paul's Cathedral, The Tower of London, The Houses of Parliament, etc. The moulds for these Christmas plates are destroyed at the end of December each year and the plates are now keenly sought after by collectors.

A series of blue and white jasperware plates was made for the celebrations of American Independence in 1976, showing six scenes of historical events that led up to the independence. The United States has a flourishing Wedgwood Collectors' Society which has commissioned several limited editions of landscape subjects for their members, and larger limited editions of 2,500 or 5,000 plates have been issued for sale in both the United States and Britain of cathedrals, castles and country houses, all produced in colour on bone china. So the tradition of landscape wares continues, encouraged by the growing number of collectors in Britain and the USA.

Windsor Castle
The first Wedgwood Christmas plate issued in 1969 and the first jasperware landscape. Diameter 8in (20.3cm).

Across the Delaware
A jasperware plate made to commemorate American Independence, 1776–1976. It shows George Washington crossing the river. Diameter 8in (20.3cm).

Appendix I

BRITISH LANDSCAPES ON BLUE-PRINTED TRANSFER WARES

The following check list of British landscapes recorded on early blue-printed wares produced in the first half of the nineteenth century gives the locality, the name of the maker or, when this is not possible, the series title e.g. *Antique Scenery*, or simply 'unattributed'. The locations listed are given the spelling most likely to be found in a modern gazetteer but this does not always correspond with the spelling in printed marks on the wares. Reference is made to the following books which illustrate some of the printed landscapes. For the sake of brevity they are referred to by the surnames of the authors.

Coysh, A. W. *Blue and White Transfer Ware 1780–1840.* 1970 (revised edition 1974) (I)
    Blue-Printed Earthenware 1800–1850. 1972 (II)
Little, W. L. *Staffordshire Blue.* 1969
Laidaker, S. *Anglo-American China.* Part 2, 1951
Moore, N. *The Old China Book.* 1935
Smith, A. *Liverpool Herculaneum Pottery.* 1970
Turner, W. (ed.) *William Adams, an Old English Potter.* 1904

Name of View	Potters who used the view
Abbey Mill	Minton miniature
Abbotsford, Roxburghshire	Bell
Ackray, Loch	John Meir & Son
Alnwick Castle, Northumberland	Adams (Little, Plate 7 and Turner, Plate XXXIV); and an unattributed view
Ambleside, Mill at	Elkins & Co.
Ampton Hall, Suffolk	A. Stevenson
Armadale, Inverness-shire	Adams
Armitage Park, Staffordshire	Clews; Wood
Armley House, Yorkshire	Hall
Arundel Castle, Sussex	*Antique Scenery*
Audley End, Essex	Stevenson
Awe, Loch	John Meir & Son (Coysh II, Plate 60)
Badminton, Gloucestershire	Hall
Balloch Castle, Dumbartonshire	Riley (Laidaker, p. 68)
Bamburgh Castle, Northumberland	Adams (Little, Plate 8)
Barcaldine Castle	John Meir & Son (Coysh II, Plate 58)
Barlborough Hall, Derbyshire	Hall; Wood
Barrington Hall, Essex	A. Stevenson
Beckenham Place, Kent	Adams
Bedfords, Essex	Wood; Unattributed
Beeston Priory, Norfolk	*Antique Scenery*
Belvoir Castle, Leicestershire	Careys; R. Stevenson; Wood
Berkeley Castle, Gloucestershire	Adams
Bickley Hall, Kent	Riley; Wood
Biddulph Castle, Staffordshire	Hall; *Antique Scenery*
Blaise Castle, Gloucestershire	Adams
Blaise Castle, Gloucestershire; Entrance to	Minton miniature
Blenheim, Oxfordshire	Adams (Coysh II, Plate 4, and Turner, Plate XLIV); Hall (Laidaker, p. 41)
Blythswood, Renfrewshire	Bell (Laidaker, p. 19)
Boreham House, Essex	A. Stevenson
Bothwell Castle, Lanarkshire	Adams; John Meir & Son
Boughton House, Northamptonshire	Hall
Bow Bridge, London	Goodwins & Harris (*Metropolitan Scenery*)
Bramber Church, Sussex	Hall
Bramham Park, Yorkshire	Adams
Brancepeth Castle, Durham	Wood (Laidaker, p. 93)
Branxholm Castle, Roxburghshire	Adams (Moore, Fig. 63)
Brecknock (Brecon), View of	Unknown
Brecknock (Brecon), Castle	Adams
Bretton Hall, Yorkshire	Riley
Brighton, Beach at	Wood
Bristol, Cook's Folly	Pountney & Allies
Harbour	Pountney & Allies
Hotwells	Pountney & Allies
River Avon	Pountney & Allies
St Vincent's Rocks	Pountney & Allies
Broadlands, Hampshire	Hall
Byland Abbey	Elkin, Knight & Co.; *Antique Scenery* (unattributed)
Bysham Abbey	Minton miniature
Bysham Monastery	Unattributed
Bywell Castle, Northumberland	Adams
Caernarvon Castle	Herculaneum (Little, Plate III)
Caistor Castle, Norfolk	Adams; *Antique Scenery*
Cambridge	Harvey; Herculaneum (Smith, Plate 169)
Caius College	J. & W. Ridgway
Clare College	J. & W. Ridgway
Downing College	J. & W. Ridgway
King's College	Harvey; J. & W. Ridgway
Library of Trinity College	J. & W. Ridgway
Pembroke Hall	J. & W. Ridgway
Senate House	J. & W. Ridgway
Sidney Sussex College	(Coysh I, Plate 69) J. & W. Ridgway
St Peter's College	J. & W. Ridgway
Trinity College	J. & W. Ridgway
Cambusnethan, Lanarkshire	Adams
Cannon Hall, Yorkshire	Riley
Canterbury Cathedral	Clews; Stevenson
Canterbury, City of	Wood
Carrick Fergus Castle and Town	Careys
Carstairs, Lanarkshire	Adams; Bell
Cashiobury Park, Hertfordshire	Adams; Hall; Wood
Castle Creke, Cork	Careys (Laidaker, p. 20)
Cave Castle, Yorkshire	Stevenson; Wood (Coysh II, Plate 128)
Chantry, Suffolk, The	Adams; A. Stevenson
Cheddar, Somerset	Clews
Chepstow Castle	Pountney & Allies
Chester	Herculaneum; Wood
Chichester, Sussex	Wood
Chichester Cathedral, Sussex	R. Stevenson
Claremont, Surrey	Wood; unattributed
Cluny Castle	Herculaneum
Cockthorpe (Cokethorpe), Oxfordshire	Hall; Wood
Colnbrook (Colnebrook), View near	Dillwyn; Goodwins & Harris
Compton Verney, Warwickshire	R. Stevenson; Wood

Conway Castle, Caernarvonshire	Hall
Corfe Castle, Dorset	Minton miniature
Coventry, Warwickshire	Wood
Cowes Harbour, Isle of Wight	Wood
Craigmullen Castle, Edinburgh	*Antique Scenery*
Creran, Loch	John Meir & Son (Coysh II, Plate 58)
Culford Hall, Suffolk	Hall; A. Stevenson (Coysh I, Plate 125)
Culzean Castle, Ayrshire	Wood
Dalguise, Perthshire	Wood; unknown
Dartmouth, Devon	Wood
Denton Park, Yorkshire	Adams (Laidaker, p. 6 and Turner, Plate XXXVIII); Hall (Laidaker, p. 44); Riley (Coysh I, Plate 77)
Dews Hall, Essex	Adams
Dilston Tower, Northumberland	Adams (Turner, Plate XLVI)
Dolbadarn (Dolberton) Tower	Unattributed
Donemark (Mealagh) Mill, Co. Cork	Clews
Donington Park	Minton miniature
Dorney Court, Buckinghamshire	R. Stevenson; Wood
Dover, Cliffs of, Kent	Wood (Laidaker, p. 106)
Dover, St Mary's	Minton miniature
Dreghorn Castle, Edinburghshire	Hall
Dublin	Harvey; Wood
Four Courts	Tams
Post Office	Tams (Little, Plate 70)
Dunolly Castle, near Oban	John Meir & Son (Coysh II, Plate 59)
Dunraven Castle, Glamorgan	Wood
Dunsany Castle, Co. Meath	Hall
Durham	Rogers (Coysh II, Plate 139); Wood
Durham Cathedral	Careys; Hall; Wood
Duston Hall, Northamptonshire	A. Stevenson
Eashing Park, Surrey	Hall
East Cowes, Isle of Wight	Wood
Eatington (Ettington) Hall, Warwickshire	Riley
Eaton Hall, Cheshire	Careys; R. Stevenson
Eddystone Lighthouse	Wood
Edinburgh	Harvey; Herculaneum; Wood
Ely, Cambridge	Wood
Embdon Castle	Minton miniature
Endsleigh Cottage, Devon	R. Stevenson
Enville Hall, Staffordshire	A. Stevenson
Erith, Kent	Wood
Esholt Hall, Yorkshire	Riley; Wood
Eton College	Phillips (Coysh II, Plate 69)
Eton College Chapel	Tams
Exeter	Wood
Faulkbourne Hall, Essex	A. Stevenson
Felix Hall	A. Stevenson
Finborough Hall, Suffolk	Hall
Floors (Fleurs) Castle, Roxburghshire	Adams (Turner, Plate XLIV)
Fonthill Abbey, Wiltshire	Adams; Clews (2 views); Hall; R. Stevenson; (Laidaker, p. 75); Wood (2 views)
Forbes Castle, Aberdeenshire	Wood
Fountains Abbey, Yorkshire	Clews (Laidaker, p. 32)
Fulham Church, Middlesex	Hall
Furness Abbey	Unattributed
Gayhurst House, Buckinghamshire	Hall
Glanbran, Carmarthenshire	Adams
Glasgow, Cathedral Church of	*Antique Scenery*
Glen Gyle, Stirlingshire & Perthshire	Clews
Gloucester	Harvey
Gloucester Cathedral	Clews
Gogerddan, Cardiganshire	Riley
Gorhambury, Hertfordshire	Hall; Stevens
Gracefield, Queen's County, Ireland	Adams
Greenwich, Kent	Clews; Harvey; Wood
Gryn, Flintshire	Hall
Gunton Hall, Norfolk	Hall; Wood
Guy's Cliff, Warwickshire	Wood
Hagley, Worcestershire	Wood
Hallow Park, Worcestershire	Unknown
Halstead, Essex	Unknown (Moore, Fig. 53)
Harewood House, Yorkshire	R. Stevenson; Wood
Haughton Hall, Norfolk	A. Stevenson
Hawthornden, Midlothian	Adams (Laidaker, p. 1 and Turner, Plate XLV)
Hereford	Wood
Hexham Abbey	*Antique Scenery* (Coysh II, Plate 134)
Hinchingbrook House, Huntingdon	Bell
Holkham Hall, Norfolk	Unattributed
Hollywell Cottage, Cavan	Adams; Riley; Wood
Holme Pierrepont Hall, Nottinghamshire	Hall
Holyrood House, Edinburgh	Wood
Houghton Conquest House, Bedfordshire	Unknown
Huntley Castle, Perthshire	Wood
Hylands, Essex	Unattributed
Invergarry Castle	John Meir & Son
Inverness	John Meir & Son
Ivybridge, Devon	Clews
Jedburgh Abbey, Roxburghshire	Adams (Turner, Plate XLV); Elkins; Stubbs; *Antique Scenery*
Katrine, Loch	John Meir & Son
Kenilworth Priory, Warwickshire	Minton miniature
Kenilworth Castle, Warwickshire	Stevenson; Wood
Kidbrook, Sussex	A. Stevenson
Kilchurn Castle	John Meir & Son
Kilcolman Castle, Co. Cork	Clews
Killin, Perthshire	Clews
Kimberley Hall, Norfolk	Unknown
Kingsweston, Gloucestershire	Riley
Kirkham Abbey	Unattributed
Kirkham Priory	Unattributed
Kirkham Priory Gateway	Unattributed
Kirkstall Abbey	*Antique Scenery*
Knaresborough Castle	Unknown
Knole, Kent	Hall
Lambton Hall, Durham	Wood
Lancaster	Elkin; Herculaneum; Rogers
Lancaster, north-east view of	*Antique Scenery*
Lanercost Priory	Minton miniature

Laxton Hall, Northamptonshire — Hall

Lechlade Bridge — Minton miniature

Leamington Baths — Unattributed

Lee, Kent — Unattributed (Coysh II, Plate 137)

Leeds, Yorkshire — Wood

Leighton Buzzard Church — Unattributed

Leven, Loch — John Meir & Son

Lichfield, Staffordshire — Careys; Wood (Laidaker, p. 87)

Lincoln — Wood

Lindertis, Forfarshire — Hall

Linlithgow Mill — Unknown

Linlithgow Palace, West Lothian — Clews, Unknown (see p. 24)

Liverpool — Wood (2 views)

Liverpool, Castle Street — Herculaneum

Llanarth Court, Monmouthshire — Hall

London, General view — Wood

Bank of England — Adams, Wood

Blackheath, view from — Goodwins & Harris

Bow Bridge — Goodwins & Harris (Metropolitan Scenery)

Church of England Missionary College — Adams

Clarence Terrace, Regent's Park — Adams; Wood

Coliseum, Regent's Park — Adams; Wood

Cornwall Terrace, Regent's Park — Adams

Covent Garden Opera House — Tams

Crystal Palace — T. Godwin

Cumberland Terrace, Regent's Park — Wood

Doric Villa in Regent's Park — Wood

Drury Lane Theatre — Tams

Dulwich College — Clews

East Gate, Regent's Park — Wood

Finsbury Chapel — Wood

Ham House — Goodwins & Harris (Metropolitan Scenery)

Hanover Lodge, Regent's Park — Wood

Hanover Terrace, Regent's Park — Adams

Haymarket Theatre — Tams

Highbury College — Adams

The Holme, Regent's Park — Adams (Turner, Plate XL); Wood

The Lake, Regent's Park — Wood

Limehouse Dock, Regent's Canal — Wood (Laidaker, p. 100 and Moore, Fig. 20)

London Institution — Adams

Macclesfield Bridge, Regent's Park — Wood

Nemcall Terrace, Regent's Park — Wood

New Post Office — Tams

North End, Hampstead — Goodwins & Harris (Metropolitan Scenery)

Opera House — Tams

Osterley Park — Ridgway; Unknown

Regent's Quadrant — Adams

Regent's Street, part of — Adams (Turner, Plate XLI)

Royal Exchange — Tams

Royal Hospital, Regent's Park — Adams

St George's Chapel, Regent's Street — Adams (Moore, Fig. 62 and Turner, Plate XLI); Wood

St Paul's Cathedral — Careys

St Paul's School — Adams (Turner, Plate XL)

St Phillip's Chapel, Regent's Park — Wood

Somerset House — Tams

Sussex Place, Regent's Park — Adams; Wood

Twickenham, View of Vauxhall Gardens — Goodwins & Harris (Metropolitan Scenery) Unattributed (see p. 26)

Villa in Regent's Park (Residence of G. B. Greenough) — Adams

Villa in Regent's Park (Residence of the Marquess of Hertford) — Adams

Villa in Regent's Park (Residence of John Maberly) — Adams; Wood

Woolwich — Goodwins & Harris (Metropolitan Scenery)

York Gate, Regent's Park — Adams

Lowther Castle, Westmorland — R. Stevenson

Ludlow Castle, Shropshire — Adams; Tams

Lumley Castle, Durham — Clews (Moore, Fig. 34)

Luscombe, Devon — Hall; Wood

Lynmouth — Unknown (see p. 28)

Maxstoke Castle, Warwickshire — Hall; Wood

Melrose Abbey, Roxburghshire — Adams; Clews

Melville Castle, Midlothian — Unknown

Menai Bridge, Anglesey — Dimmock (Coysh II, Plate 27)

Mereworth House, Kent — A. Stevenson

Monmouth — Unknown (Coysh II, Plate 136)

Morpeth Castle, Northumberland — Adams

Murthley, Perthshire — Adams

Nant Mill, Caernarvonshire — Elkin, Knight & Co.

Netley Abbey, Hampshire — Unattributed

Newark, near — Elkin, Knight & Co.

Newnham Court, Oxfordshire — Unknown

Newstead Abbey, Nottinghamshire — Baker, Bevins & Irwin

Normanton Park, Rutlandshire — Adams (Laidaker, p. 3)

Norwich, Norfolk — Clews; Wood

Norwich Cathedral, Norfolk — Hall

Nottingham — Clews

Oatlands, Surrey — Hall; A. Stevenson

Oich, Loch, Inverness-shire — Meir

Orielton, Pembrokeshire — Wood

Orwell Park, Suffolk — Riley; Unknown

Oxburgh Hall, Norfolk — Davenport (see p. 30) R. Stevenson (see p. 30) Wood

Oxford — Harvey; Herculaneum (Smith, Plate 165); Pountney & Allies (Coysh II, Plate 72)

All Soul's College and St Mary's Church — J. & W. Ridgway (Moore, Fig. 43)

Christ Church — J. & W. Ridgway (see p. 31)

Christ Church (a different view) — J. & W. Ridgway

Observatory — J. & W. Ridgway

Redcliffe Library	J. & W. Ridgway (Little, Plate 51)
Theatre Printing House	J. & W. Ridgway (Coysh I, Plate 70)
Trinity College	J. & W. Ridgway
Wadham College	J. & W. Ridgway
Pains Hill, Surrey	Hall (*see* p. 32)
Painshanger, Hertfordshire	Hall
Park Place, Herley	Pountney & Allies
Pass of the Trossacks	John Meir & Son
Peterborough, Huntingdonshire	Wood
Pishiobury, Hertfordshire	Adams
Plas Newydd, Anglesey	Adams
Powder Mill, Hastings	Unknown (Coysh II, Plate 135)
Richmond	Unattributed
Richmond, view of	Goodwins & Harris (*Metropolitan Scenery*); Wood
Richmond Bridge	Harvey (Little, Plate 8); Pountney & Allies (*see* p. 32)
Ripon, Yorkshire	Clews; Unknown
Rivaulx Abbey, Yorkshire	Clews
Roche Abbey, Yorkshire	Unknown
Rochester, Kent	Wood
Rochester Castle, Kent	Clews; Wood
Rode Hall, Cheshire	Adams; Hall
Rookery, The, Surrey	Adams; Riley; Wood
Ross Castle, Monmouthshire	Wood
Rothesay Castle, Bute	Clews
St Alban's Abbey, Hertfordshire	Unknown
St Alban's Castle, Prison	Hall
St Catherine's Hill, near Guildford	Adams (Turner, Plate XXXIX); Clews
St Wolston's, Co. Kildare	Hall (Laidaker, p. 46)
Salisbury, Wiltshire	Wood
Saltwood Castle, Kent	Wood
Saxham Hall, Suffolk	Unknown
Scaleby Castle, Cumberland	Adams
Shirley House, Surrey	Wood
Shrewsbury, Shropshire	Herculaneum (Smith, Plate 162)
Shugborough Hall, Staffordshire	Careys; Hall
Slingsby Castle, Yorkshire	Unknown
Southampton, Hampshire	Wood
Stirling Castle, Perthshire	*Antique Scenery*
Stratford-on-Avon, Warwickshire	Clews
Summer Hall, Kent	A. Stevenson
Sunninghill Park, Berkshire	Adams
Sutton Court, Herefordshire	Wood
Sutton Hoo, Bedfordshire	Careys
Sweetheart Abbey	Elkin, Knight & Co. (Coysh II, Plate 138)
Taymouth Castle, Perthshire	Riley; Wood
Teddesley Hall, Staffordshire	Unattributed
Tewkesbury Church, Gloucestershire	Minton miniature
Thornton Abbey, Lincolnshire	Clews
Thornton Castle, Staffordshire	Wood
Thorpe, Derbyshire	Unknown
Thrybergh Hall, Yorkshire	Wood
Tintern Abbey, Monmouthshire	Clews
Tixall Hall, Staffordshire	Adams; Hall
Tonbridge Castle, Kent	A. Stevenson

Trentham Hall, Staffordshire	Mason (Plate *see* p. 35)
Valle Crucis Abbey, Denbighshire	Hall
Virginia Water, Surrey	A. Stevenson
Walsingham Priory, Norfolk	A. Stevenson
Wanstead House, Essex	A. Stevenson
Wardour Castle, Wiltshire	Wood (2 views)
Warkworth Castle, Northumberland	Clews
Warleigh House, Somerset	Hall
Warwick Castle	Elkins; Wood (Moore, Fig. 21)
Welcombe, Warwickshire	Wood
Wells Cathedral, Somerset	Adams; Clews; Wood
Westacre House, Norfolk	Hall
Whitby Harbour, Yorkshire	Adams (Turner, Plate XLVI); Wood
Wilderness, Kent	Hall
Windermere Lake, Westmorland	R. Stevenson
Windsor Castle, Berkshire	Adams; Clews (Laidaker, p. 30); Goodwins & Harris (*Metropolitan Scenery*); R. Stevenson; Wood
Windsor Park, King's Cottage	Riley
Wingfield Castle, Suffolk	*Antique Scenery*
Wiston Hall, Leicestershire	Hall; Riley
Witney, Oxfordshire	Unknown
Woburn Abbey, Bedfordshire	Careys
Wolseley Hall, Staffordshire	Unknown
Wolvesley Castle (Abbey), Hampshire	Adams; A. Stevenson
Worcester	Herculaneum; Wood
Worcester Cathedral	Hall; Tams
Writtle Lodge, Essex	A. Stevenson
Yarmouth, Isle of Wight	Wood
York	Wood
York Cathedral (Minster)	Careys; Henshall; Mason; Rogers; R. Stevenson
York, St Mary's Abbey	Adams; Clews

Appendix II

NORTH AMERICAN LANDSCAPES ON
STAFFORDSHIRE EARTHENWARES
(Note: Slightly different titles have NOT been recorded, but
the generally recognized geographic name is listed.)

Name of view	Potters who used view
Albany, NY	J. & J. Jackson; Charles Meigh; Mellor, Venables & Co.; W. Ridgway & Co.; James and Ralph Clews

(Attributed to James and Ralph Clews as maker of the 'City
Series' *Antiques*, March 1954, p. 238; *Antiques*, February
1974, p. 324.)

Capitol	R. Stevenson
City Hall	Unknown
City of, State of NY	Enoch Wood & Sons
Dutch Church	R. Stevenson (*see* p. 56)
Fort Frederick, State St from Van Rennselair Island	Wedgwood
	Wedgwood

Old State Capitol — Wedgwood
Schuyler House on the Flats — Wedgwood
Theatre — Unknown
Theatre (1824) — R. Stevenson
Thorps & Sprague — Unknown
Allegheny Scenery — Bell
Altoona (Pa); Horse Shoe Curve — Wedgwood; Rowland & Marsellus

(This New York firm was actually the importer rather than the maker, but they have now come to be known as 'R & M' plates. *Antiques*, September 1942, p. 155.)

American Villa — Unknown, marked 'B.B. & B.'

Amherst (Mass.); Mt Pleasant Classical Institution — James and Ralph Clews

Anthony's Nose — W. Ridgway
Arlington (Va); Home of Martha Custis — Wedgwood

Ashville (NC); Baltimore House — Rowland & Marsellus

Bakers Falls, Hudson River — James and Ralph Clews
Ballston Springs, NY — Charles Meigh
Baltimore, Md — James and Ralph Clews; Thomas Godwin; Charles Meigh; Mellor Venables & Co.; W. Ridgway

Alms House — Unknown
Assembly Rooms — Unknown
Battle Monument — J. & J. Jackson
Court House — S. Henshall (*see* p. 63) and Unknown
Exchange — S. Henshall; J. & W. Ridgway
Holliday Street Theatre — S. Henshall (*see* p. 63)
Hospital — Unknown
Masonic Hall — Unknown
Belleville on the Passaic River — Enoch Wood & Sons
Beverly, Mass., Hetmere — Wedgwood
Birmingham Meeting House — Minton
Boston, Mass. — Charles Meigh; Mellor, Venables & Co.
Almhouse — J. & W. Ridgway; R. Stevenson
Athenaeum — J. & W. Ridgway; R. Stevenson
Bunker's Hill — T. Godwin
Bunker's Hill Monument — J. & J. Jackson; Rowland & Marsellus; Wedgwood
Court House — J. & W. Ridgway; R. Stevenson
Faneuil Hall — Rowland & Marsellus; Wedgwood
from the Dorchester Heights — C. Meigh; W. Ridgway
Green Dragon Tavern — Wedgwood
Hancock House — J. & J. Jackson (*see* p. 45)
Hospital — J. & W. Ridgway, R. Stevenson
Insane Hospital — J. & W. Ridgway
Kings Chapel, 1686 — Wedgwood
Lamb Tavern, 1746 — Wedgwood
Lawrence Mansion — R. Stevenson
Mitchell & Freemans China & Glass Warehouse — Adams (*see* p. 44)
Nahant Hotel, near — R. Stevenson; Stubbs (*see* p. 47)
New Library — Rowland & Marsellus
Octagon Church — J. & W. Ridgway; R. Stevenson

Old Brick Church, 1713 — Wedgwood
Old Corner Book Store — Wedgwood
Old Feather Store, 1680–1868 — Wedgwood
Old North Church, 1775 — Rowland & Marsellus; Wedgwood
Old South Church, 1793 — Rowland & Marsellus; Wedgwood
Old State House, East End, 1712 — Wedgwood
Old Sun Tavern, 1690–1895 — Wedgwood
Old Theatre, 1794 — Wedgwood
Park Street Church — Wedgwood
Public Library — Wedgwood
St Paul's Church — J. & W. Ridgway
State House — J. & J. Jackson; Minton (*see* p. 46); J. & W. Ridgway; Rogers; Rowland & Marsellus; R. Stevenson; Stubbs; Wedgwood; Enoch Wood & Sons
State Street & Old State House — Wedgwood
Town House, 1657–1711 — Wedgwood
Trinity Church — Wedgwood
Brooklyn, NY
Ferry — T. Godwin; R. Stevenson
from Gowanus Heights — Mellor, Venables & Co.; W. Ridgway
Buffalo on Lake Erie, NY — Enoch Wood & Sons
Caldwell, Lake George, NY — T. Godwin; C. Meigh; Mellor, Venables & Co.; W. Ridgway
California
Carmel Mission — Wedgwood
San Fernando Rey Mission — Wedgwood
San Gabriel Archangel Mission — Wedgwood
San Luis Rey de Francia Mission — Wedgwood
Santa Barbara Mission — Wedgwood
Cambridge
College, Mass — J. & W. Ridgway
Washington Elm, 1775 — Rowland & Marsellus, Wedgwood
Catskill Mountain
House — Adams; J. & J. Jackson; Enoch Wood & Sons
Hudson River — Enoch Wood & Sons; Andrew Stevenson
Village of Catskill — W. Ridgway
Cedar, St Lawrence (Mass.), Village of — T. Godwin; F. Morley
Centre Harbor (NH) Sawmill at — W. Ridgway
Charleston (SC) Exchange — J. & W. Ridgway (*see* p. 66); R. Stevenson
Chester, Pa
Old Court House — Minton
The Pusey House, near — Minton
Chillicothe, Ohio — James and Ralph Clews
Cold Spring (NY); Undercliff near — W. Ridgway
Cleveland, Ohio
Cuyahoga County Soldiers' & Sailors' Monument — Wedgwood
Garfield Memorial — Wedgwood

Subject	Maker
Columbia Bridge on the Susquehanna	W. Ridgway
Colorado Springs, Col.; The Antlers	Wedgwood
Columbus, Ohio	James and Ralph Clews
Concord, Mass.; Old North Bridge	Wedgwood
Conway (NH), View near	Adams; J. & J. Jackson
Crow Nest from Bull Hill	J. & J. Jackson
Delaware Water Gap, Pa	W. Ridgway; Rowland & Marsellus
Denver, Colorado; State Capitol	Wedgwood
Detroit, Mich.	James and Ralph Clews
Duxbury, Conn.	
John Alden House	Rowland & Marsellus
Miles Standish House	Rowland & Marsellus
East Port	T. Godwin; W. Ridgway
Erie Canal	
at Buffalo, NY	R. Stevenson
entrance into Hudson at Albany	Enoch Wood & Sons
Fishkill, Hudson River	James and Ralph Clews (*see* p. 54)
Fort Conanicut, RI	J. & J. Jackson
Fort Edwards, Hudson River	Adams; James and Ralph Clews
Fort Griswald	Rowland & Marsellus
Fort Miller, Hudson River	James and Ralph Clews
Fort Montgomery, Hudson River	James and Ralph Clews
Fort Putman, Hudson River	W. Ridgway
Fort Ticonderoga	J. & J. Jackson
Framingham, Mass.; Memorial Hall	Wedgwood
Germantown, Pa	
Chew House, 1777	Minton
Old Academy	Minton
Gilpin's Mill on the Brandywine Creek	Enoch Wood & Sons
Glenns Falls, NY	James and Ralph Clews
Governors Island	R. Stevenson
Greensburg, NY; Tappen Zee from	Enoch Wood & Sons
Hadley's Falls, NY	James and Ralph Clews
Hallowell, Bay of Quinte	F. Morley
Harpers Ferry	Adams
from the Potomac side	W. Ridgway
Harrisburg, Pa; Capitol at	Tams; Wedgwood
Haverhill, Mass.; Birthplace of Whittier	Wedgwood
Hartford, Conn.	J. & J. Jackson
Deaf & Dumb Asylum	J. & W. Ridgway; R. Stevenson
First Church	Wedgwood
State House	R. Stevenson
Harvard College, Cambridge, Mass.	James and Ralph Clews; J. & J. Jackson; R. Stevenson; Enoch Wood & Sons (*see* p. 46); Unknown
Harvard University, Mass.	J. & J. Jackson; Enoch Wood & Sons
Headwaters of the Juniata	Adams
Highlands, Hudson River	Enoch Wood & Sons
at West Point	Enoch Wood & Sons
near Newburgh	Enoch Wood & Sons
North River	Stubbs
Hingham, Mass.; Old Meeting House, 1681	Wedgwood
Hobart town, NY	James and Ralph Clews
Hoboken, NJ	Stubbs
Holyoke, Mass.; Summit House, Mt Tom	Wedgwood
Hope Mill, Catskill, NY	Enoch Wood & Sons
Hudson City, NY	C. Meigh; Mellor, Venables & Co.
Hudson, NY	W. Ridgway
Hudson River, near	James and Ralph Clews
Hurl Gate, East River, View at	Stubbs
Jessup's Landing, Hudson River	James and Ralph Clews
Kingston, Lake Ontario	Podmore, Walker & Co.
Kosciusko's Tomb	W. Ridgway
Lake George, NY	Adams; J. & J. Jackson, Enoch Wood & Sons
View of the road to	R. Stevenson
Lake Memphremagog (Vt), Outlet of	T. Godwin
Little Falls, NY	W. Ridgway
Aqueduct Bridge	Unknown
at Luzerne, Hudson River	James and Ralph Clews
Mohawk River	J. & J. Jackson
Lincoln, Neb.; State Capitol	Wedgwood
Louisville, Ky	James and Ralph Clews
Marine Hospital	Enoch Wood & Sons (*see* p. 68)
Lowell, Mass.; City Hall	Rowland and Marsellus
Marietta, Ohio; Campus Martius	Wedgwood
Mendenhall Ferry	Stubbs
Meredith, NH	W. Ridgway
Minnehaha Falls, Minnesota	Wedgwood
Montmorenci Falls	Enoch Wood & Sons (*see* p. 58)
Montreal, Canada	Davenport (*see* p. 57) Podmore Walker & Co.
Mount Ida, View from	C. Meigh
Mount of Holy Cross, Colorado	Wedgwood
Mount Vernon, NY	J. & W. Ridgway; Royal Doulton (*see* p. 65); Rowland & Marsellus; Wedgwood; Enoch Wood & Sons; Unknown
Washington's Tomb	Mellor, Venables & Co.; Unknown
Nantucket, Mass.; Old Mill	Wedgwood
Narrows,	
from Ft Hamilton	T. Godwin; W. Ridgway
from Staten Island	W. Ridgway
Lake George, NY	W. Ridgway
Natural Bridge, Virginia	Enoch Wood & Sons
Nauvoo, Ill.; Mormon Temple	J. Twigg & Co. (*see* p. 67)
Navy Island, Canada	Podmore, Walker & Co.
Newburgh, NY	James and Ralph Clews; J. & J. Jackson; Enoch Wood & Sons
Washington Hqs.	Wedgwood
Ruggles House, View from	W. Ridgway
New Haven, Conn.	J. & J. Jackson
State House	Enoch Wood & Sons
Yale College	T. Godwin; J. & J. Jackson; C. Meigh; Wedgwood
New London, Conn.	
Old Nathan Hale School House	Wedgwood
Old Town Mill	Wedgwood
New Orleans, LA	R. Stevenson
Newport (RI) Old Stone Mill	Rowlands & Marsellus (*see* p. 48)

Place	Maker
Newton, NJ Residence of Richard Jordon	
New York City	J. Heath & Co. (see p. 59)
Almshouse	Adams; J. & J. Jackson; C. Meigh; J. & W. Ridgway; R. Stevenson; A. Stevenson
American (Scudder's) Museum	R. Stevenson (see p. 52)
Battery	R. Stevenson; Enoch Wood & Sons
Bay	Stubbs; Enoch Wood & Sons
Castle Garden	Enoch Wood & Sons (see p. 52)
Catholic Cathedral	A. Stevenson
Church (Murray Street)	A. Stevenson
Church (Dr Mason's)	Stubbs
City Hall	James and Ralph Clews; J. & J. Jackson; J. & W. Ridgway; A. Stevenson; R. Stevenson; Stubbs (see p. 51)
City Hotel	R. Stevenson
Coenties Slip, Burning of	Unknown
Columbia College	A. Stevenson; R. Stevenson (see p. 53)
Esplanade & Castle Garden	R. Stevenson
Federal Hall	Rowland & Marsellus
Fort Gansevoort	R. Stevenson
from Heights near Brooklyn	A. Stevenson (see p. 50)
from Staten Island	Enoch Wood & Sons
from Weehawk	A. Stevenson; J. & J. Jackson; Mellor Venables & Co.
Fulton Market	R. Stevenson
Grants Tomb	Wedgwood
Hospital	R. Stevenson
Hudson River	James and Ralph Clews
Insane Asylum	James and Ralph Clews; R. Stevenson
Merchants' Exchange	Unknown (see p. 53)
Park Theatre	John Geddes; R. Stevenson; Stubbs
St Patrick's Cathedral, Mott St.	R. S. Stevenson
St Paul's Chapel	R. Stevenson
Niagara, NY	Adams; Rowland & Marsellus; R. Stevenson
from the American side	Enoch Wood & Sons (see p. 57)
suspension bridge and whirlpool rapids	Rowland & Marsellus
Table Rock	Enoch Wood & Sons
Northampton, Mass.	C. Meigh
Ontario, Lake Scenery	J. Heath
Pass in the Catskills, NY	Enoch Wood & Sons
Passaic Falls, NJ	Enoch Wood & Sons
Peekskill Landing, Hudson River	W. Ridgway
Philadelphia	James and Ralph Clews
Bank of the US	Stubbs (see p. 61)
Bartram House	Minton
Betsy Ross House	Minton
Carpenter's Hall	Minton
Christ Church	Minton
Custom House	J. & W. Ridgway
Deaf and Dumb Asylum	J. & J. Jackson; Enoch Wood & Sons
Fairmount	Stubbs
Girard's Bank	J. & J. Jackson
Girard College	Minton
Independence Hall	Minton; Rowland & Marsellus; Wedgwood
Library	J. & W. Ridgway (see p. 60)
Masonic Hall	J. & W. Ridgway; R. Stevenson
Old Swedes Church	Minton
Pennsylvania Hospital	J. & W. Ridgway (see p. 60); R. Stevenson
Race Street Bridge	J. & J. Jackson; Enoch Wood & Sons
Staughtons Church	J. & W. Ridgway; R. Stevenson
Sweet Briar	Minton
United States Hotel	Tams (see p. 61)
Water works and Dam	Henshall (see p. 62); Minton; J. & J. Jackson; R. Stevenson
William Penn's Cottage	Minton
William Penn's Treaty Tree	Minton
Woodlands, near	Stubbs
Pikes Peak from the Garden of the Gods, Colorado	Wedgwood
Pine Orchard House, Catskill, NY	Enoch Wood & Sons
Pittsburgh, Pa	James and Ralph Clews
Penitentiary in Allegheney, near	James and Ralph Clews
Pittsfield, Mass.	
Maplewood Hotel	Wedgwood
Old Elm Park	Wedgwood
Onota Lake	Wedgwood
Wendell Hotel	Wedgwood
Winter view of	James and Ralph Clews
Plymouth, Mass. in 1622	Wedgwood
Plymouth Rock	Rowland & Marsellus
Portland, Maine	
Birthplace of Longfellow	Wedgwood
Longfellow's Early Home, 1785	Wedgwood
State Street Church	Wedgwood
Quebec, Canada	James and Ralph Clews; Podmore, Walker & Co.; Enoch Wood & Sons (see p. 58); Unknown
Quincy, Mass., Adjacent Lean-to Houses	Wedgwood
Radnor, Pa; Old St Davids	Minton
Residence of	
Late Richard Jordan, NJ	J. Heath
S. Russel NY	Enoch Wood & Sons
Riceborough, Georgia	R. Stevenson; Enoch Wood & Sons (see p. 67)
Richmond, Virginia	J. & J. Jackson
Rideau Canal, Bytown (Ottawa)	F. Morley & Co.
Rochester; Aqueduct Bridge	R. Stevenson
Sacandaga & Hudson Rivers, Junction at	A. Stevenson; James and Ralph Clews
Salem, Mass.	
First Church	Wedgwood
House of the Seven Gables	Wedgwood
Witch House	Wedgwood
Salt Lake City, Utah; Mormon Temple Block	Wedgwood
Sandusky, Ohio	James and Ralph Clews
Sandy Hill, Hudson River	James and Ralph Clews
Saugerties (NY); Ironworks	J. & J. Jackson
Savannah (Ga); Bank	J. & W. Ridgway
Schenectady on the Mohawk River, NY	Adams; J. & J. Jackson
Schuylkill Water Works	T. Godwin; C. Meigh
Shannondale Springs, Va	Adams; J. & J. Jackson; J. & W. Ridgway

Shipping Port on the Ohio,
  Kentucky   Enoch Wood & Sons;
                                    R. Stevenson
Springfield, Ill.; Lincoln's   Wedgwood
  Home
St Augustine, Florida
  Old City Gate   Rowland & Marsellus;
                                    Wedgwood
  Watch Towers of San   Wedgwood
    Moro
Stenton, Pa.   Minton
Sudbury, Mass., The   Wedgwood
  Wayside Inn
Sunbury House on the   Minton
  Neshaminy
Swarthmore, Pa.; The West   Minton
  House
Transylvania University,   Enoch Wood & Sons
  Lexington, Ky
Trenton Falls, NJ   Enoch Wood & Sons
Troy, NY   W. Ridgway
  from Mt Ida   James and Ralph Clews;
                                    A. Stevenson
University of Maryland   Enoch Wood & Sons
Upper Ferry Bridge over the   Stubbs (see p. 62)
  River Schuylkill
Utica, NY   T. Godwin; C. Meigh;
                                    W. Ridgway
Valley Forge; Washington's   Minton; Rowland &
  Hqs, NY   Marsellus
Valley of the Shenandoah   W. Ridgway
  from Jefferson's Rock, Va
Valley of Wyoming Pa   W. Ridgway
Vevay, Indiana   S. Henshall
Wadsworth Tower, Conn.   A. Stevenson; Enoch Wood
                                    & Sons

Washington, DC   Adams; James and Ralph
                                    Clews; C. Meigh; Enoch
                                    Wood & Sons
  Capitol   T. Godwin; C. Meigh; J. &
                                    W. Ridgway (see p. 64);
                                    W. Ridgway; Rowland &
                                    Marsellus; R. Stevenson;
                                    Tams; Enoch Wood &
                                    Sons; Wedgwood
  Department of State   Enoch Wood & Sons
  Library of Congress, 1897   Wedgwood
  President's House   T. Godwin; J. & J. Jackson;
                                    W. Ridgway; Enoch Wood
                                    & Sons (see p. 65)
  White House   Mellor, Venables & Co.;
                                    Rowland & Marsellus;
                                    Wedgwood; Enoch Wood &
                                    Sons
Weehawken (NJ), Near   W. Ridgway
West Center (Pa), Old Court   Minton
  House
West Point, NY   James and Ralph Clews
  Military Academy   Enoch Wood & Sons
  Military School   Adams (see p. 55)
White Mountains, NH   Adams
White Sulphur Springs,   J. & J. Jackson
  Ohio
Wilkes-Barre, Vale of   W. Ridgway
  Wyoming, Pa
Wilmington, Del.; Old   Minton
  Swedes Church
Wooding Station on the   Enoch Wood & Sons
  Mississippi
Wrights Ferry on the   James and Ralph Clews
  Susquehanna